D1527562

THE GARY SCHOOLS

THE FROEBEL SCHOOL, GARY, INDIANA

A model Wirt school-plant, with all grades, from kindergarten through the High School
Social center and people's university. Built 1913

THE GARY SCHOOLS

RANDOLPH S. BOURNE

Epilogue by
Abraham Flexner and Frank P. Bachman
Introduced and annotated by
Adeline and Murray Levine

THE M.I.T. PRESS
Cambridge, Massachusetts, and London, England

Reproduced from The Gary Schools *by Randolph S. Bourne, published by Houghton Mifflin, Boston, 1916, and* The Gary Schools: A General Account *by Abraham Flexner and Frank P. Bachman, published by the General Education Board, New York, 1918.*

Set in Monotype Scotch Roman, and printed and bound in the United States of America by The Riverside Press, Inc.

ISBN 0 262 02066 1 (hardcover)

Library of Congress catalog card number: 70-118344

"... for in this school idea, which I really believe is the biggest thing in the country today, everything is significant of everything else and won't be cut off into pieces and still live."

R. S. Bourne, June 25, 1915

CONTENTS

ACKNOWLEDGMENTS

We are indebted to a number of people for their assistance in developing the manuscript. Myles Slatin, Director of Libraries at the State University at Buffalo, read and criticized in great detail an earlier version of this manuscript. He helped us clarify the expression of our ideas and was also of great assistance in locating source material, particularly since both of us are relatively new in the field of history. This manuscript is in many ways a product of the Yale Psycho-Educational Clinic under the direction of Seymour B. Sarason, to whom we are indebted for his comments and encouragement. Warren Button of the Social, Philosophical, and Historical Foundations Department of the Faculty of Educational Studies at Buffalo also read the manuscript and offered helpful comments. Warren Bennis, Vice-President for Academic Affairs at Buffalo, recognized the value of reprinting the Bourne book and helped us to elicit the interest of our publisher. David and Zachary Levine were, as always, helpful in letting us know when we were becoming two great bores on the subject of Gary.

In Gary, Superintendent of Schools Gordon McAndrews and his staff were most hospitable and cordial, making people, records, and buildings available to us. Mr. H. Theo. Tatum, Mrs. Gertrude Ward, and Mrs. Gladys Pierce contributed valuable memories about the earlier days of the Gary system. Mrs. Shroll, Librarian of the Indiana Room of the Gary Public Library, gave us the benefit of her extensive knowledge of local history and led us to the critical sources.

The Wirt Manuscripts are located in the Lilly Library of Indiana University in Bloomington. The kindness and efficiency of Elfrieda Lang and her staff at the Lilly Library made our work immeasurably easier.

The Bourne Manuscripts are located in the Butler Library of Columbia University and are available on microfilm. Columbia University has given us permission to publish the excerpts from Bourne's correspondence.

We are also appreciative of the assistance provided by a small award from the Committee for the Distribution of Institutional Funds of the Faculty of Social Sciences and Administration which partially covered travel expenses in connection with this venture. We would have had considerably more difficulty in doing this job were it not for the hospitality of various Cutlers and various Smiths. We are appreciative also of the secretarial help provided in both the Department of Psychology, especially by Erma Rawlings, and the Department of Sociology at the State University at Buffalo in completing the manuscript.

Adeline Levine
Assistant Professor of Sociology
Murray Levine
Professor of Psychology
State University of New York at Buffalo
November 20, 1969

INTRODUCTION TO THE NEW EDITION

The Gary Schools, a Sociohistorical Study of the Process of Change

Adeline and Murray Levine

THE GARY SCHOOLS, by Randolph Bourne, deserves renewed attention because it provides a detailed description of an important innovation in school curriculum, method, and organization. It describes a public school system in an urban, industrial community, built on the concept that school is a life in itself, beyond its significance as preparation for life. In Gary, Indiana, an effort was made to have the school day filled with a program of work, study, and play; an effort was made to relate the work of the school both to the community within its walls and to the larger community the schools served. In this book the reader will find the concepts of a relevant education, a learning community, an educational park, a community school, and team teaching. The Gary system provided for diverse interests and aptitudes and tried to prevent the failure of children who could not perform well in the usual school's circumscribed and prescribed program.

The ideas developed in Gary, Indiana, as early as 1906 were far more advanced than many educational proposals made today. The book, for that reason, contributes to discussions of contemporary social problems. William Wirt, Gary's first school superintendent, proposed that schools be built in or near parks; that the city's museums,[1] libraries, zoos, gardens, and playgrounds be integral parts of the school; that they be available to *all* members of the community, on the basis of an extended day, week, and year. Wirt was advocating efficiency in the use of public facilities, but he was offering a prescription to counter the alienation of schools from their communities as well. Schools that welcomed the adults and children who wanted to study and play day and night, instead of locking them out at three o'clock, made the people of a community feel that the schools were their own. *The*

[1]To this day the corridors of the Froebel and Emerson schools are lined, not with the usual semispontaneous paper collages, but with many carefully chosen, well-framed oil paintings.

Gary Schools is witness that our schools can be more than they are.

Bourne wrote this book because the Gary school system had achieved national and international recognition in its day. Part of our introduction is devoted to putting the Gary system into the context of that day. Aspects of the Gary program were successfully adopted by literally hundreds of communities. There were frequent problems of the sort inherent in any large-scale enterprise, but in some cities, notably New York, efforts to "Garyize" the schools met with disaster.

Some of the leading figures of the day took an interest in the renowned Gary system. We are fortunate that the program was the subject of an evaluation more intensive than Bourne's, which informs us of some of the problems of innovation within a school system.[2] Abraham Flexner had earlier estab-

[2]The Gary Schools were internationally known; famous people of the day were involved, and William Wirt was in New York on a part-time basis, carrying out his consultancy in part through the mails. For these reasons, there is a rich source of material (in newspapers and preserved correspondence particularly in the Wirt papers, located in the Lilly Library of Indiana University) about the political and social problems involved in large-scale institutional change.

lished his reputation when he evaluated medical education in the United States. In February 1916 he undertook a study of the Gary school system under the auspices of the Rockefeller-funded General Education Board. The results of that study were published in eight volumes, one of which was a summary called *The Gary Schools: A General Account.* Sections of Flexner's evaluative study of the Gary Schools are included here as an epilogue to Bourne's more enamored account. The reader may enjoy testing his own acumen in predicting the kinds of problems and deficiencies noted in the evaluative study after reading Bourne's description.

The Author

Randolph Bourne (1886–1918) is of interest as an author, for he preceded today's cultural radicals in his views. With exquisite sensitivity, his articulate essays revealed the inner state of youth in the urban, industrial society in which he lived. When he described his own sensations, he gave his contemporaries words with which to conceptualize their experiences and thus helped them to interpret themselves in relation to their times.

A champion of life, he stated the cause of the vigorous youth who opposed the archaic institutional molds which were holding and shaping them in the images and icons of the past. But his was not a negative voice; he was neither a muckraker nor an alarmist. He was not a biting satirist, mocking the manners of his times, although he could have been that, and he certainly possessed appropriate intellectual tools in his wit, perceptiveness, and eagerness to engage in sophisticated intellectual combat. Rather than waste himself in attack, however, he stated the positive case for enjoying to the fullest that "poignant consciousness of being alive," that "great, rich rush and flood of energy" at the base of the overpowering urge toward self-expression, an urge that would not then and cannot today be realized in the forms and symbols of the past. It is in this sense that he was a cultural radical, interested in the possibilities for life in the modern world, and it was in this spirit that he interested himself in the schools of his time.

Bourne grew up in Bloomfield, New Jersey, a combination of small town and suburbia, where his early life inadvertently prepared him for his later career.[3] A stunted hunchback with one side of his face distorted, he was perforce an outsider, a marginal man, despite his intellectual precociousness and musical talent. His aristocratic, well-to-do family claimed American ancestry dating back to 1628; however, his own father was an unsuccessful "magazine agent" who probably drank too much.[4]

[3]This account draws heavily on Moreau's (1966) detailed biography of Bourne, although the interpretation is our responsibility.

[4]On the paternal side, Bourne's great-grandfather was an abolitionist and his grandfather a minister, precisely the background of the social workers of the late nineteenth and early twentieth centuries. Davis (1967) has suggested that the newly rising business class was successfully competing at that time with the traditional professions for prestige and power. In a society in which the economy was expanding and shifting rapidly, both the possibilities and the uncertainties of life were on the increase for young people. Having a father who succeeded neither at business nor in a profession, Bourne, lacking a career model, had both the psychic freedom to pursue his own way in the world and necessity to do so. If one looks at the father's unsuccessful career as a dried-up tributary, so to speak, in the continuity from past to future, then one can better appreciate Bourne's commitment to the "Experimental Life" and his flexibility in enthusiastically seeking new cultural forms.

Bourne's life in Bloomfield was traditional indeed; he was brought up in a Calvinist home and educated in a small private school where spinster teachers vainly attempted to repress his mind's desire to grow. He felt starved for intellectual nutriment in a home in which "The classics were enshrined behind glass doors that were very hard to open." There was no money to send him to college, and upon graduation from high school in 1903 he tried to find a place in the business world. Here he experienced fully the humiliation and defeat awaiting the handicapped when they attempt to be part of a world that does little to conceal its revulsion for deformity. A short time with an exploitative manufacturer of player piano rolls, followed by an uncertain career as a music teacher and accompanist, gave Bourne sufficient experience with that "real world" to impel him to follow the advice of a friend and apply for a scholarship at Columbia. At the age of twenty-three he became an undergraduate.

Columbia in the early 1900s was the land of his people. Academic stars in law and literature, in history and political science, in anthropology, sociology, psychology, philosophy, and education provided a stimulating intellectual atmosphere in which the old was criticized and reinterpreted, and the new was created. Bourne's agile, absorbent mind thrived at Columbia. His first article, on the generation gap, was published in the *Atlantic* when he was a sophomore. He followed it shortly with several other pieces, a considerable achievement for a college student. In addition, he contributed frequently to the *Columbia Monthly*, the undergraduate literary magazine, and became its editor. He was a member of Phi Beta Kappa, and after graduation he stayed on for an M.A. in sociology, writing a sociological description of the suburban community of Bloomfield for his thesis.

In 1913 he won a fellowship enabling him to tour Europe for a year. The trip gave him another perspective on the old and the new. When he returned to the United States, rather than take up an academic career, he began work as a free-lance writer. He had some assurance of support from Herbert Croly, the editor of the newly organized

New Republic, to whom Bourne had been recommended by Charles Beard. By the time of his death in 1918, the *New Republic* had published some 120 of Bourne's articles.

Estimates of Bourne's position in the world of letters and his influence on his contemporaries may be found in a number of sources. Biographies by Filler (1943) and Moreau (1966) and essays by Van Wyck Brooks (1956), Lasch (1965), and Paul (1966) are all highly appreciative of him as a writer, critic, social philosopher, conversationalist, and friend. Wherever he was he livened the atmosphere with music and with conversation sparkling with ideas. In the brief span from 1913 to 1918 he made his mark on the New York intellectual community, exposing the educated public to fresh ideas about life and thought through his numerous essays, articles, and reviews in the *New Republic* and similar journals.

Bourne was one of the most outspoken critics of the First World War, a war whose degree of unpopularity is surprising from our contemporary perspective. Outraged by the government's attempt to suppress dissent (at this time such democratic heroes as

Teddy Roosevelt and Woodrow Wilson were suggesting that war dissenters were traitors), Bourne increasingly wrote in opposition to the war. He was also working on a manuscript, *The State* (Bourne, 1946), in which he argued that governmental forms were necessarily repressive. He seemed to be moving toward an increasingly radical political position, anticipating today's radicals in both his social and his political outlook. His death in the influenza epidemic of 1918 shocked his friends and moved him into the status of culture hero and martyr for a brief period afterward.

Bourne wrote in a context surprisingly similar to our own time in social history. His rediscovery in the last few years has meaning primarily because he *was* so sensitive an instrument, expressing so well the feelings of those seeking to throw off the cultural bonds that seem to inhibit the freedom of expression and fullness of life style that a postindustrial, postscarcity society could afford for everyone.

Schools in the Modern Age

Social philosophers, in the quest to influence their culture, inevitably turn to the education of the young. Thus it was with Bourne. Let us glance at the forces affecting American schools at the turn of the century.

By the early 1900s, the balance in this country had already shifted away from a rural and agrarian life to an urban, industrial existence. The post–Civil War industrial expansion had produced factories, railroads, and cities and had created major shifts in the social structure. A new class of entrepreneurs and technicians moved rapidly to dominate all facets of American life. At the same time, huge forces of foreign laborers were transplanted into the grimy, teeming slums and into the mushrooming apartment dwellings and housing tracts that eventually turned suburb into city and city into megalopolis.

Some newly spawned industrial cities lacked social institutions; in some cities, they were incipient; in those places where institutions had developed in an earlier day, they were irrelevant. In some cities, among the working class, the symptoms of alienation were manifest in suicide, in crime and delinquency, in divorce and desertion (Levine and Levine, 1970). Among the children of the well-to-do, alienation took the form of rootlessness, a sense of being useless, which turned some to an interest in the Bohemian life and others to a career of social and cultural reform (Addams, 1910).

In an earlier day American public education, particularly at the secondary school level, was geared to a time when the educated man was the minister, the lawyer, the doctor, the wealthy merchant, or the banker (Katz, 1968). The curriculum emphasized formalized presentation of the classics, the ideals and the instrumentalities of the past. The rudiments of reading, writing, and arithmetic sufficed for the everyday needs of most men. Industrial development in the second half of the nineteenth century meant that more and more people lived in the cities and worked in factories away from home; in an increasingly complex world parents could no longer teach children how to earn their living as adults. Compulsory school attendance laws, often passed in conjunction with child labor regulations, brought all children into the schools and attempted to keep them there. American public education faced the problem of accommodating the increasingly varied educational requirements of an increasingly heterogeneous population. Accommodation meant change — change in what the schools were teaching, to whom, and how. The demand for change was expressed in an idiom quite familiar to our present day. Schools were to become more relevant to the conditions of modern industrial life.

That simple statement obscures a great deal, for far-reaching changes in the school curriculum reflect changes in the culture, in our beliefs about what is important, about what ought to be preserved, about how we ought to live. Reformers wanted to modernize the curriculum to include science, government, home economics, shop, industrial and business training, and recreational arts. They were saying that what was taught in the past was no longer pertinent. They were also indirectly asserting that social dominance had been achieved by the new class of industrial kings and the associated coterie of educated managers, engineers, and scientists. The modern industrial organization was pouring forth material wealth at a prodigious rate, and what was good for the new industrial state, for its managers and workers, was now to be preserved by preparing children to take a part in that world.

Agitation for school change had begun in the 1870s with one important movement focusing on the introduction of vocational education into the curriculum. A prime mover in this direction from an early date, was the National Association of Manufacturers, concerned that workers be prepared for the factories and interested in wresting control of apprenticeships from the men on the line (Cremin, 1961).

As the immigrants poured into the cities, the schools' problems increased. The schools were inadequate for the discipline, health, and delinquency problems and evidences of family disorganization that came to their direct attention. Humanistically oriented social reformers, captivated by a concept of the sacredness of the child, hoped that school change would provide the means to relieve human suffering. Those who believed that progress required freedom from the cultural strictures and authoritarian dicta of the past saw the path to far-reaching social change in modification of the way children were trained to live. John Dewey said in *My Pedagogic Creed* (1897): "I believe that education is the fundamental method of social progress and reform." To learn by doing forced one toward empirical values and away from a reliance on the authority of the priests of the past culture. Thus, a strange alliance for progress was formed between industrialists and the keepers of the new culture — the writers, sociologists, social philosophers, and reformers.

The national struggle for school change was centered in the larger cities where industrial problems were most acute. The schools of Gary, Indiana, molded together the piecemeal solutions found in many schools throughout the nation. In Gary the varied trends toward change were put together in a showcase school system, throughout a whole city, and that city combined the very best and worst of modern industrial life.

The Setting for the Gary Schools: Gary, Indiana

Gary, Indiana, was built to order in 1906. It was the midwestern base for the most modern of manufacturing complexes, a huge technical miracle worthy of the first billion-dollar corporation, United States Steel. The steel city was named for Elbert H. Gary, the Indiana farmboy who grew up to be the first Chairman of the Board of United States Steel. As the legal counsel for steel companies, Gary convinced J. P. Morgan and John D. Rockefeller that the day of the robber baron was over and that a trust, merging and coordinating powerful interests, would produce predictable progress, while free competition between industrial giants would lead only to a mutually disastrous standstill (see Cotter, 1921; Gulick, 1924; and Tarbell, 1926).

While the mills and the residential and business areas were being constructed, the region that was to become Gary was a wild and woolly frontier town. Gun-toting men nightly drank and brawled themselves into insensibility. A handful of women cared for their families in a settlement of tents under the most rugged conditions. Other females were few in number; some made their way by working in bawdy houses, others by caring for the construction crews in boarding houses and tents, often set up in polyandrous fashion (Moore, 1959).

Within ten years substantial houses for skilled workmen, clerical and executive personnel, ancillary business and professional men were located on the side of the tracks green with newly planted lawns and trees. On the other side of the tracks, unrestricted by the niceties of any enforced building code, land speculators and profit-hungry housing contractors covered the sandy ground with a motley collection of houses and shacks for the laborers. Numerous saloons, bawdy houses, and gambling dens served the recreational needs of the rugged laborers, including immigrants from thirty countries. In those first dozen years, politics was a rough-and-tumble game. When election day arrived in 1913, it was a point of local pride that the state militia needed only to be kept on alert and not be called out to maintain order. As Bourne pointed out, these problems differed in degree, not in kind, from those of any other American city of the time. They were, however, rather more acute for having been compressed in a somewhat smaller area and having been telescoped in time as well.

Despite its problems, Gary was the Magic City of Steel where youth came to make their fortunes. One rarely met a person over thirty-five in the city. Here, previously unimaginable financial resources were combined with industrial know-how, executive talent, and science in the creation of an industrial plant. Those who came to Gary, who bought property there, or who established businesses and professions there identified with the wealth, the power, and the unlimited optimism of the largest corporation in the world. To maintain the land and construction boom and to maintain the labor supply, it was necessary for the city to attract more of the right kind of people who would develop its social institutions.

Wirt and His School System

In this boomtown atmosphere, the brilliant William Wirt (1873–1938) was the first superintendent of schools. Born on an Indiana farm, Wirt held an appointment as superintendent of schools in a small town while he prepared for admission to the bar at the age of twenty-one. A few years later he obtained a college degree from DePauw University. With a reputation as an educational innovator in his previous post, Wirt came to Gary in 1906, impressing the Mayor and the three school board members with his ideas. The board members were a civil engineer, a surveyor who helped to build the steel mills and city, and a railroad engineer. Not only did Wirt's educational ideas appeal to the optimism of the managers of Gary, but when he argued that schools should be engineered for maximum efficiency, he invoked an almost sacred concept. Using charts, tables, and figures persuasive to engineers and managers, Wirt showed how his plan could produce more classes at a lower cost, while including innovative features in curriculum and methods, in school building, and in the relationship of the schools to other community resources. Wirt was evidently exceptionally impressive both intellectually and emotionally, and he used this persuasiveness to quickly convince the town managers to remodel the school they had already built and to build two magnificent new plants, the Emerson and the Froebel schools.[5]

Once Gary's modern progressive system was in operation, its fame spread very quickly. Either Wirt's adroit management of professional relationships or national interest in the city of Gary may have been responsible, but at any rate a combination of a network of professional contacts and a few laudatory articles in nationally circulating popular magazines made Gary famous in educational circles throughout the land. By 1911 teachers, administrators, school board members, journalists, social reformers, and other interested citizens visited the Gary schools in such numbers that special arrangements were necessary to accommodate them.

[5]The growth and development of the Gary school system is worth noting, for the fact that Wirt started from scratch does not tell the whole story. While he did not introduce change into an ongoing system, he still had to win the support of the economic and political power structure; the school administrators, who were largely of his own selection; teachers, many of whom were adventurous people who came to work in a new city; the body of parents, among whom Wirt was established as a parent himself and as one of the community's leading citizens and businessmen; the newspapers, with which he managed excellent relations; and the children, for whom he helped to make school an enjoyable place. In short, he designed and administered schools to truly serve their community, and he was of that community.

Classroom visitations were limited to four weekly periods during the year, and during each period as many as 600 people observed the schools in action. Visiting privileges were requested from all over the country and from several foreign countries as well. Reciprocally, Wirt received innumerable invitations to address a variety of groups of citizens and professionals and to consult in school systems around the country.

Wirt's ideas, as well as their presentation and implementation, struck a responsive note in people at large. Insofar as we can judge from letters, newspaper reports, and magazine articles, the generally adulating tone of Bourne's book matched the feeling of most of those who viewed or heard about the Gary program.

Bourne and the Gary Schools in New York

Bourne cannot be credited with popularizing the Gary idea, for the system had achieved international recognition long before Bourne published his first article on public education in the *New Republic* in 1914, and well before he went to Gary in the spring of

1915.[6] In order to understand the place of this book (and the articles, for they are really inseparable), it is necessary to digress into a discussion of Bourne's sponsorship and the social and political forces they represented.

Bourne had become the education writer for the *New Republic*, a "Journal of Opinion," as soon as Willard and Dorothy Whitney Straight established it in 1914. Herbert Croly, the first editor, believed fiercely in the promise of American life. Although the journal was critical of certain aspects of

[6]P. P. Claxton, United States Superintendent of Education had sent the distinguished educators W. P. Burris (Wirt's predecessor in Bluffton, Indiana, incidentally) and Harlan Updegraff to visit in 1912 and in 1913, with approval expressed officially in an Office of Education document published in 1914 (Claxton, 1924). A year before Bourne began writing about Gary, Evelyn Dewey had come to visit as her father's emissary and the Gary system then received the imprimatur of the high priest of progressive education (Dewey and Dewey, 1915). In August 1915 recognition was capped by a medal for an exhibit on the Gary schools at the International Panama Pacific Exposition in San Francisco. The exhibit, financed by United States Steel, was conceived by Wirt and operated by his representatives. Literally hundreds of school systems eventually adopted all or part of the Gary system or took inspiration for their own school reforms from Gary. There is a remarkable example of the diffusion of innovation in the story of how the Gary plan spread throughout the land, whether or not one agrees with the form in which the innovation spread (Callahan, 1962).

American life, it was not a radical publication. Instead, it supported the best of modern American culture, voicing the opinion of the new class of educated technologists who were to break away from the older forms of American culture while standing foursquare behind the American system. The sponsorship of the *New Republic* helps to explain why, as a matter of editorial policy, the journal was critical of the schools as they existed and was ready to give important support to the Gary school plan when the plan was introduced into New York City.

In 1913 John Purroy Mitchel was elected Mayor of New York on a Republican-Fusion ticket, promising to rid municipal government of the corruption of Tammany and to infuse city hall with honesty and efficiency. As part of Mitchel's program, the Gary plan was intricately involved with politics from the very beginning and played an important part in his administration. When Mitchel took office in 1914, the city was faced with a financial crisis alleviated by a loan arranged by J. P. Morgan in cooperation with most of the large investment banks in the city. A condition of the loan was that New York establish a pay-as-you-go plan. Thus, the city could borrow money for self-liquidating subways, but not to replace schools, long since antiquated and overcrowded (Lewinson, 1965).

By late 1913 the Gary school system attracted the interest of the socially prominent and the intellectual elite who supported the municipal and social reform movement of the early 1900s. Leading New York citizens visited Gary and invited Wirt to speak in their city at both private and public meetings. In June 1914 Mayor Mitchel visited the Gary schools, accompanied by a party including T. W. Churchill, the President of the Board of Education, and Henry Bruere, the City Chamberlain. Later that month Mitchel, Churchill, and City Comptroller William Prendergast all endorsed the introduction of a vocational education program; that fall Wirt was hired as a consultant on a one-week-a-month basis at a fee of $10,000 a year. Clearly, aspects of the Gary system were to be introduced into the New York system. The efficient Gary plan promised huge savings in capital construction and operating costs, as well as providing modern education.

The Public Education Association (PEA) was a prime force seeking this particular reform in the schools. Its leadership of powerful bankers, corporation lawyers, socialites, and a few professionals with access to money had supported Mitchel in 1913 and were to go all out for him again in 1917. According to Cohen (1964), Dorothy Whitney Straight was preeminent among those who subsidized the PEA; her husband, Willard Straight, who helped to nominate Mitchel for Mayor in 1913, was also an active member of the PEA (Lewinson, 1965).

We have no evidence that Willard and Dorothy Whitney Straight were directly involved, as publishers, in the decision to ask Bourne to write the series of articles on the Gary system for the *New Republic*.[7] It

[7]Bourne's unqualified enthusiasm for the Gary system was perfectly genuine. He advocated the release of youth from the inappropriate and repressive institutions of a past society and culture (Bourne, 1913). The Gary system, a marked departure from tradition, represented the full implementation of the concepts of Bourne's intellectual and philosophical hero, John Dewey. For Bourne to write enthusiastically about the Gary system was fully in keeping with all else that he did and wrote.

should be underscored, however, that the publication of Bourne's articles in the *New Republic*, and later the book, coincided precisely with the public campaign and attendant political pressure to introduce a version of the Gary system into New York City.

Bourne's endorsement of the Gary idea seemed to have had two important effects. First, Bourne effectively reached the solid middle class who voted regularly, who were a step or two below the wealthy and the aristocrats, but whose affluence was tied to the system that was supporting them in increasingly good style. He could help to shape their beliefs and give voice to their concern about developing a modern culture. Wirt himself wrote to Bourne and attributed to Bourne's writings much of the progress in introducing the Gary plan into New York.[8]

Second, and more subtly pertinent to the New York scene, his endorsement and the *New Republic* editorial endorsement gave the proponents of the Gary system credibility in the eyes of the intellectual elite, who would read or believe little that was

[8]Letter to R. S. Bourne from W. A. Wirt, July 2, 1915.

produced by one who was not an approved member of the New York establishment.

The solid connections with the magazine writers, critics, editors, and editorial assistants enabled proponents of the Gary plan to maintain a generally good press and appease, if not suppress, critics of the plan when opposition arose.[9]

Resistance to the Gary Plan in New York

At first it seemed there would be something satisfactory for everyone: a school curriculum attuned to an urban, industrial community, taught in the modern, progressive style, while utilizing existing resources. The Mitchel administration was so committed to the Gary plan that by 1916 approval of the Board of Education budget was made contingent upon an agreement to "Garyize" the entire school system.

However, there was immediate resistance to the Gary plan. Professional jealousy, resentment aroused by the interference of society ladies and politicians, the attempt

[9]See letters from Alice Barrows-Fernandez to William Wirt, July 22, 1915; October 29, 1915; November 17, 1915.

to guard professional prerogatives, and the undesirable features of the New York version all influenced the school administrators who opposed and sabotaged the implementation of the plan. The professional administrators were also motivated by a desire to eliminate Wirt from consideration as a candidate for the superintendency when the aging incumbent retired. City teachers opposed the system, partly from an instinctive aversion to change and partly as a reaction to administration criticism of the efficiency of teachers. With good reason they feared that the installation of the Gary system in New York would be at their expense, for the administration had been hostile to their concerns about pensions and salaries. In the fall and winter of 1915 there was a brief but heated controversy about provisions for released time for religious education. Anticlerical feelings and arguments for the separation of church and state met head on with the usual pieties about providing for religious education for youth.

In the 1917 mayoralty election, Tammany ran an undistinguished, obscure judge, John

F. Hylan, against Mitchel. A strong socialist candidate and a regular Republican completed the field. Hylan in particular hit the school issue hard. Labor unions drew effectively on stored-up anger against the capitalists, for the name of Elbert Gary was associated with the plan. Two Rockefeller employees, Abraham Flexner and Raymond Fosdick, were Gary plan supporters on the New York Board of Education, a fact enabling its opponents to persuade immigrant parents that the plan's intent was to prepare their children for the factories. The presence of society ladies on the speaking platform in favor of the plan did not help.

There were many sources of resentment against Mitchel and his administration. He seemed to favor the very wealthy; he had fought against raises for teachers and other city employees; inflation struck in 1917, sending food prices soaring, and his administration's response was unsympathetic and ineffectual. Mitchel campaigned on a preparedness ticket at a time when there was much antiwar sentiment (Lewinson, 1965).

The smoldering resentments flared up

during the latter part of October 1917 in week-long riots centered in the schools of upper Manhattan, the Bronx, and Brooklyn. Primarily they were protests against the attempt at "Garyizing." Throughout the week children formed into mobs, going from school to school, trying to disrupt activities. Armed with sticks, stones, and bottles, they smashed windows, fought the police, and regrouped every time they were dispersed. Some of the worst of the disorders occurred in the Williamsburg and Brownsville sections of Brooklyn, where at the height of the trouble 10,000 children and their parents marched and demonstrated.

The disorders occurred in Jewish neighborhoods, and most of those arrested, as reported in the newspapers, bore Jewish names. Parental aspirations for children had been threatened by the Gary plan, and deep-seated resentment was elicited. The concept of community control was invoked. One newspaper reporter's account of an uproarious mass meeting during the strike included a paragraph that seems to sum up a great deal:

> One mother cried out from the platform against the Gary system, shouting: "We want our kinder to learn mit der book, der paper und der pensil [*sic*] und not mit der sewing and der shop!" Another aroused the parents with a vehement denunciation of what "they are doing mit unserer kinder. Dey are unserer kinder, not theirs." The law compelled them to send their children to school and when they had asked that this Garyizing not be done they were not listened to; but it was done [*The Globe and Commercial Advertiser*, October 18, 1917].

There was never any official investigation of the disorders, for two weeks later Hylan had won an overwhelming election victory. Some said that Tammany had agitated the disorders, while others said they were promoted by socialists and radicals, but such widespread and long-lasting disruption cannot be attributed to the work of agitators alone. There were legitimate grievances, which the Gary supporters had tried to deny. The program was installed with inadequate preparation of facilities, and before teachers and principals had been properly trained. Many of the children and their parents had but the vaguest ideas of the Gary plan goals; clearly, the school authorities had not communicated with their constituency, and they had ignored the pleas of the resistant parents. Among Hylan's first statements after election was a reaffirmation that the Gary plan would be abolished, and upon assuming office, he issued orders to stop further changes, and to undo what had already been done. Hylan responded to the mandate of his constituency, and the disorders ceased. Thus, the support of the Mayor's office, control of the Board of Education, the support of a large segment of the power structure, and a favorable press were insufficient to ensure that far-reaching changes in the school could be implemented. The resistance of the school administration, the teachers, and parents was a greater force and blocked the Garyizing of the New York schools.

The Style of the Book

The subject matter of Bourne's book is clarified by examining it in the context of ongoing social change; so too can the very style of the book be better understood. Bourne, as indicated previously, undertook the Gary work willingly, traveling to Gary early in 1915, writing articles in the *New Republic*, and elsewhere describing the Gary system enthusiastically. However, the book itself presents a puzzle. In the words of Filler, "*The Gary Schools* was an unpretentious work, written in straight reportorial style, and giving the facts and features of the Gary system as Bourne had observed them." The writing style was uncharacteristic of Bourne, as Filler observed: "*Education and Living*,[10] on the other hand, was a rich volume of essays, everywhere brightened by personal impressions and reminiscences" (Filler, 1943, p. 68).

Why was *The Gary Schools* so different and so uncharacteristic a book for Bourne? Bourne apparently initiated the idea for the book, and when he took it to Houghton Mifflin, his previous publisher, the editor of the Education Department readily accepted Bourne's suggestion. Bourne worked at a lovely summer retreat in Dublin, New Hampshire, an artist's colony set idyllically

[10]A later book, it included some of the *New Republic* Gary articles in their original form and other educational essays (Bourne, 1917).

near Monadnock Mountain. He settled comfortably on a little dock in the summer sunshine[11] but unaccountably had great difficulty in writing the book. Bourne, whose correspondence was filled with exquisitely refined expressions of his personal impressions and experience, wrote as follows to a friend and fellow contributor to the *New Republic*, Elizabeth Shepley Sergeant:[12]

> I have spent a week trying to make a book out of my Gary articles, floundering most dreadfully and getting myself surrounded by a mass of loosely collected notes and reflections in all stages of importance. Houghton Mifflin have agreed to look at it, but I think they will demand something less impressionistic than my articles. I find it almost impossible to say anything without assuming that my reader knows all about the details of the organization I'm supposed to be explaining. Some of my friends even had trouble with the articles. Is it really possible to combine facts and figures in the tone that you feel the thing in? If I let go of my tone for a moment, I drop into something worse than flatness. I'm really having a difficult time and I can hardly feel that labor will help me out. Even an orderly outline won't do much, for in this school idea, which I really believe is the

[11]Letter to E. S. Sergeant, August 9, 1915. The Bourne papers are in the Butler Library of Columbia University.

[12]Letter from R. S. Bourne to Elizabeth Shepley Sergeant, June 25, 1915.

biggest thing in the country today, everything is significant of everything else and won't be cut off into pieces and still live. I know it will seem too poetical for the publisher, and I will have wasted a summer in working at the futile thing. I admire order and precision immensely and it makes me angry not to achieve it in a subject about which I am so enthusiastic. And there is every motive to do the book, that of spreading the good news, and the sordid one of making a book that will appeal. . . .

As he continued writing, however, Bourne's frustrations only grew, and, upon finishing the manuscript, he wrote:[13]

I finished it in a wild burst of speed on Saturday, and had to pay with a lame back which has kept me sitting around with pillows ever since. . . . The Gary work is a fearful thing. I tried to be official and descriptive and to quench all unqualified enthusiasm with the result that I am duller than the most cautious schoolman. . . . Can one do these things without blushing. I shall never touch Gary again. . . .

Even after *The Gary Schools* was published, Bourne was distressed by its "banality," and he longed to do "some slashing work" in his role as an education expert.[14]

[13]Letter to E. S. Sergeant, September 23, 1915.
[14]Letter to Alyse Gregory, January 21, 1916.

Why was he distressed about his presentation of the Gary system, and why did it have the form it had? The answer might lie in part in the demands his publisher and editor made of him. Their demands were prompted by their estimate of the appropriate market for the book. Houghton Mifflin, an established, respected publishing house, was a leader in the educational publishing field, and the educational market was to become an important factor in Houghton Mifflin's growth, for by 1930 the Education Department was twelve times its size in 1900, with an annual business larger than all the other selling departments put together. The Education Department was under the editorship of F. S. Hoyt, a graduate of Yale and Columbia, for many years a teacher, a public school administrator, and a professor of education at the college level before assuming his duties at Houghton Mifflin. He was a man who could be presumed to know the attitudes of the schoolman. At that time Houghton Mifflin was beginning to exploit the new market, as described in a history of its educational department.

> Shortly after 1910, the divergent current of professional reading began to flow off in another direction. Teachers colleges and normal schools sprang up, and many leading educators determined that those teachers who lack genius and ingenuity at least should not lack a knowledge of good methods of instruction. Professional books on teaching and on administration were demanded both for training courses and for the use of teachers and administrators [Houghton Mifflin, 1930, p. 15].

The exploitation of that market, rather than political considerations, was probably involved in Hoyt's directions to Bourne about how the Gary book was to be written.[15] In an early letter, Hoyt stated that the *New Republic* articles would have to be considerably modified, if not rewritten entirely, so that the description of the system could be taken up in a logical order and points of interest to superintendents and teachers could be developed. In particular, he urged that Bourne remove or tone down the "eulogy of Mr. Wirt."[16]

After Bourne had submitted some early

[15]Houghton Mifflin was listed as a large contributor to Mitchel in the 1917 mayoralty campaign (Lewinson, 1965).

[16]Letter from F. S. Hoyt to Randolph S. Bourne, June 2, 1915.

chapters, Hoyt wrote that he felt the material was sufficiently developed "so that the ordinary superintendent and teacher can grasp the essential features of the Gary system." He continued to point out the problems in writing for a particular market and in relation to a particular set of critics:[17]

> May we caution you about being too eulogistic of Mr. Wirt, not that we do not appreciate his qualities of leadership, and the constructive work he has done in Gary, but in the judgement of many school men his type of school has not yet been sufficiently tested to justify the country in accepting his educational ideas and ideals as worked out in Gary . . . . We recognize of course that whatever has been most successfully accomplished has often had persistent and destructive criticism aimed at it until its success was demonstrated beyond doubt. The point in making this suggestion is that in writing a book which is to be a permanent affair, it is well to be somewhat conservative in estimating present social movements that have not become firmly established. We realize that we are presenting a very trite matter to you, but we believe that your enthusiasm for Mr. Wirt which we confess we share, may lead you to bring his personality into too great prominence. . . . Although you do not send us the material for Chapter II, the outline for this chapter indicates that the

[17]Letter from F. S. Hoyt to Randolph S. Bourne, July 22, 1915.

> readers of this book who are desirous of learning exactly what is being accomplished in Gary may not care to read about such topics as: Failure of recent attempts to improve conventional schools; efforts inadequate because partial work on the reform of the traditional school . . .

What we have here is evidence that the author's natural inclinations were curbed and directed by an editor's estimate of appropriate material for a particular audience. One point of interest is the subjective sense of dissatisfaction and difficulty Bourne had in writing the book. Although all of the material was on hand, and much of it already written up for publication in separate articles, the creative process was limited, not by any deep-seated neurotic conflict, as we are led to expect in "writer's block," but rather by the demand to write in an uncongenial style. Bourne wrote the book partly for the income, but more because of his desire to spread "the good news" to that audience of teachers and administrators he perceived as the prime obstacles to the implementation of school reform.[18] The paradox

[18]Bourne, 1916; Bourne, undated autographed manuscript; Bourne papers, Box 3, Columbia University Collection.

lies in the fact that he would attempt to persuade, not in his own spontaneous and effective manner, but in an uncongenial style that led to a book that was clear, but uninspiring.

The editor's role is of considerable interest.[19] His suggestions were harsh; he was very directive about the selection and presentation of appropriate material. Why did he not want Bourne to write in his own effective style if he commissioned Bourne to do the work? Clearly, the editor offered more than minimal guidance for a piece of work. Was Hoyt only making an estimate of what would sell to a particular audience, or did he also act as an agent or advocate, so to speak, for the interests of a particular audience? Did Hoyt, a man who must have had career identification with professional educators, have some conviction about what *should* be the form of a work to be sold to teachers and professional educationists?

[19]We are indebted to Professor George Huaco for pointing out some of these relationships to us. Huaco, taking his lead from Escarpit (1960) and Watt (1962) writing about the novel, has demonstrated similar phenomena for the film (1965) and for a group of Mexican novelists of the revolution (in press).

Bourne's usual audience was the modern man, the educated professional or executive, appreciative of his world, desirous of developing cultural forms that would permit him a greater level of affective expression. Today, the child of the middle and upper-middle classes becomes the cultural radical. Just so, it is likely that the new affluence of that time attracted those who wanted to express themselves freely in a world very different from that of their parents and grandparents. It is no accident that Bourne used the gospel phrase "spread the good news," for he wrote that instrumentalism, Deweyian and Jamesian pragmatism, was indeed his religion (Bourne, 1956). C. Wright Mills has also pointed out that the pragmatic and instrumental philosophy, emphasizing experimentation and trial, was attractive to that class (Mills, 1964).

Bourne's emotionally expressive, poetical style would have presented no problem to the usual reader of the *New Republic.* Hoyt, on the other hand, represented two other groups of interests. One was the teachers, and the other the professional administrators. Both of these groups would have been attracted by a different, more precise, and more orderly form. Teachers in general tend to come from a less affluent sector than do executives and other professionals. Frequently they are upwardly mobile, the first generation within their own families to have any postsecondary education. The upwardly mobile interests of the class of teachers would have been best served by a predictable reality enabling the group to know how to proceed and how to safeguard its own interests.[20] Moreover, the beginnings of professionalism may be seen in the early 1900s. There were very few teachers' colleges and normal schools in the country in 1900, but many by 1930. A free-flowing, impressionistic study could not convey the specifics of the skill of teaching to the aspiring educator. The teachers' colleges, attempting to rationalize an enforced separateness from the liberal arts colleges, probably needed professional jargon and mystifying tables to

[20]In this interpretation, we disagree with Mills (1964), who has probably overemphasized the attraction progressive principles have for the ordinary teacher.

establish expertise and exclusive control of the profession (Sarason, Davidson, and Blatt, 1962).

The situation of the professional administrator was related but somewhat different. The professional administrator's interests would best be served by establishing his independence in matters of curriculum, methods, and hiring from the politically dominated school boards. The administrator, too, was under some pressure to show that he was as proficient a scientific manager as his counterpart in the business world (Callahan, 1962). For his purposes, a literary form that was precise, orderly, scientific, rational, and nonemotional would serve best. If he were to be administrator of an orderly world, he would have to think in a precise and orderly way. A "poetical" version of what was presented as a major modern efficient application of scientific management of the schools would have been almost a contradiction in terms.

Even in the very writing of the book then, in the matter of the schools, ". . . everything is significant of everything else and won't be cut off into pieces and still live." We hope that those concerned with wide-scale innovation in the schools will find useful ideas in *The Gary Schools*, but we also hope they seriously consider the massive problems encountered in changing a major cultural institution.[21]

[21]One of the best statements of the problem of changing schools may be found in Seymour B. Sarason's forthcoming book, *The Culture of the School and the Problem of Change* (in press).

PREFACE

The public school system of Gary, Indiana, has attracted during the last few years the general attention of progressive educators all over the country as perhaps the most ingenious attempt yet made to meet the formidable problems of congested urban life and modern vocational demands which are presented to the administrators of the city school. A broad educational philosophy has combined with administrative skill to produce a type of school which represents a fundamental reorganization of the public school to meet changing social and industrial conditions. A new balance of school activities, an increased wealth of facilities, the opening-up of opportunities to the younger children, the institution of a new kind of vocational training, the fusing of activities into an organic whole so that the school becomes a children's community, the correlation of school activities with community activities, and lastly, the application of principles of economics to public school management which permit greatly increased educational and recreational facilities not only for children in the schools, but also for adults, — these are the features of the Gary school system that have aroused the enthusiasm of many educators, and made it one of the most visited and discussed school systems in the country. Dr. David Snedden, Commissioner of Education in Massachusetts, has said that the system of education at Gary "more adequately meets the needs of city children than any other system of which the writer has knowledge." Professor John Dewey declared recently, at a public meeting in New York City, called to discuss the adoption of the Gary plan in the New York schools, that "no more important question affecting the future of the people of New York has come before them for many years." The United States Bureau of Education in 1914 published a report on the Gary schools, made after "a careful and prolonged study at first hand" extending over a period of two years. In this report Commissioner P. P. Claxton records his belief that "the superintendent and board of education of the Gary schools have succeeded in working out plans for a more economic use of school funds, a fuller and more effective use of the time of the children, a better adjustment of the work of the schools to the condition and needs of individual children, greater economy in supervision, a better correlation of the so-called 'regular work' and 'special activities' of the school, a more practical form of industrial education, and at a cost less nearly prohibitive than is usually found in public schools in the cities of this country."

Schools in many towns and cities in all parts of the country have been reorganized on the Gary plan or have been experimenting with it. The Gary plan has been introduced in the schools of small cities such as Sewickley, Newcastle, and Swarthmore, Pennsylvania; Kalamazoo, Michigan; Winetka, Illinois. Kansas City has been experimenting with it. The Chicago authorities have recently pronounced their two years' experiment an unqualified success. Passaic, New Jersey, has a highly successful Gary school in operation. In Troy, New York, the authorities are reorganizing the entire school system on the Gary plan. In New York City two schools were operated for most of the school year, 1914–15, Superintendent Wirt of Gary having been called in to supervise the reorganization and advise the Board of Education in their attempt to meet the "part-time" problems in congested school districts. As a result of this experiment the Board of Education has recently decided to extend the Gary plan to two school districts in the Borough of the Bronx, involving fourteen schools and 46,000 pupils. Superintendent Wirt has presented figures to show that, by the adoption of the Gary plan and the expenditure of only $5,000,000 (the cost of a dozen school buildings which would provide at the maximum for 20,000 children), the New York authorities could practically relieve their part-time situation which now involves 132,000 children. Not only has the success of the Gary plan been striking in the larger cities, but it has proved its adaptability to the small school as well. Three of the schools of Gary are practically rural schools in outlying districts, but the principles of the Gary plan are found applicable there as well as in the recently erected model school plants. The flexibility of the plan, the ingenuity and soundness of its economical and educational principles, its feasibility of imitation, and adaptation to communities the most diverse, makes its discussion one of national significance.

The material on the Gary plan has been generally confined to bulletins, magazine articles, and educational reports. One of the best discussions of the Gary school is to be found in a chapter of Professor Dewey's recent book, which contains, in addition, the educational theory and historical background upon which the Gary plan has been worked out by Superintendent William Wirt, himself a pupil and disciple of Dewey. I give here a list of the Gary material which I have used. Some of it is generally available, some not. I am much indebted to these investigators. I have even plagiarized from myself.

Books and Bulletins:—

John Dewey and Evelyn Dewey: *Schools of To-Morrow.* New York: E. P. Dutton & Co.

William Paxton Burris: *The Public School System of Gary, Indiana.* Bulletin of the United States Bureau of Education (1914), No. 18. (To be obtained free of charge from the Commissioner of Education, Washington, D.C.) An excellent and very enthusiastic report of a long investigation of the Gary schools.

Graham Romeyn Taylor: *Satellite Cities.* New York: D. Appleton & Co.

Chapters VI and VII of this book contain a comprehensive account of the history and social conditions of the city of Gary up to date.

Magazine articles:—

John Franklin Bobbitt: "The Elimination of Waste in Education." *The Elementary School Teacher,* February, 1912.

Charles S. Coons: "The Teaching of Science in the Gary Schools." *School and Society,* April 17, 1915. Able discussion of the philosophy which motivates Gary education, by the teacher of chemistry in Froebel School, Gary.

Raymond Dean Chadwick: "Vitalizing the History Work." *History Teachers' Magazine,* April, 1915. By the history teacher in the Emerson School, Gary.

Randolph S. Bourne: "Schools in Gary"; "Communities for Children"; "Really Public Schools"; "Apprentices to the Schools"; "The Natural School." Five articles in the *New Republic,* March 27, April 3, April 10, April 24, May 1, 1915. A more impressionistic survey of the schools based on a personal visit in March, 1915.

Reports: —

William Wirt: *A Report on a Plan of Organization for Coöperative and Continuation Courses.* Department of Education, City of New York.

The Reorganization of Public School 89, Brooklyn, New York. Report made January 19, 1915, to President Thomas W. Churchill, Board of Education, New York City.

Report upon a Proposed Reorganization for Public Schools 28, 2, 42, 6, 59, 44, 5, 53, 40, 32, 4, and 45, The Bronx, New York City.

These three reports are invaluable as a discussion of the philosophy and technique of many of the features of the Gary plan, discussed by the Gary Superintendent of Schools.

Alice Barrows-Fernandez: *A Reply to Associate Superintendent Shallow's* [of New York City] *Report on the Gary Schools.* Published by the author, 35 West 39th St., New York City.

A valuable document, with a wealth of figures and authoritative discussion of current misconceptions regarding the work of the Gary schools.

R. S. B.

September 1915.

INTRODUCTION

During the past fifteen years I have tried approximately fifty different programs for "work-study-and-play schools." The several factors in such a school program can be combined in countless ways. I have not tried to design a system or type of school program as a set form that would constitute a universal ideal school for all children. Rather, I have tried to develop a system of school administration that would make possible the providing of a great variety of school types, so that all cities and all of the children in the several parts of a city may have the kind of school they need.

I have had only two fixed principles since I began establishing work-study-and-play schools at Bluffton, Indiana, in the year 1900.

First: All children should be busy all day long at work, study, and play under right conditions.

Second: Cities can finance an adequate work-study-and-play program only when all the facilities of the entire community for the work, study, and play of children are properly coördinated with the school, the coördinating agent, so that all facilities supplement one another and "peak-loads" are avoided by keeping all facilities of the school plant in use all of the time.

At what children work, study, and play; how they work, study, and play; when and where they work, study, and play; what facilities are provided for work, study, and play; and the total and relative amount of time given to work, study, and play; — these may vary with every city and with every school in a city. No set system can possibly meet the needs of all children, nor could a set system be uniformly provided with the existing child-welfare facilities.

It is not desirable or possible uniformly to establish one particular scheme of departmentalizing work between teachers or of rotating classes between different types of facilities. The only important thing is so to departmentalize teaching and so to rotate classes that the teachers may render the greatest service with the least expenditure of energy, and that the maximum use may be secured from the school plant and other child-welfare facilities.

WILLIAM WIRT.

THE GARY SCHOOLS

I

THE COMMUNITY SETTING

To set the Gary schools in their proper perspective, one must discount at the start any prevailing impression that the distinctive traits are due to peculiar local conditions, or to the enlightened philanthropy of the United States Steel Corporation, which founded the town in 1906 as the site for its new plant, the most complete system of steel mills west of Pittsburg. For to the steel officials the building of the town was incidental to the creation of the plant. Gary in consequence is far less of a "satellite city" than other made-to-order towns. The opportunity to plan the city, provide fundamental necessities for community life, determine the character of the housing, and predestine the lines of growth, all in the best and most enlightened way, was taken advantage of by the Steel Corporation only in part. Very little of the marvelous science and engineering skill that went into the making of the steel plant went into the even more important task of creating a model city. Several hundred houses were built, it is true, for the skilled labor and officialdom of the plants, but practically no attempt was made to house the low-paid unskilled labor. The result has been the development of large tracts by land speculators, and all the problems of congestion and bad housing and sanitation that curse the larger industrial cities. The connection of the Steel Corporation with the town has been throughout that of any land and development company. Communal problems have all been thrown upon the people themselves to solve. The new community was incorporated as soon as possible as a municipality under the laws of the State of Indiana, and has organized all its municipal functions, including the public schools, in entire independence of the Steel Corporation, with which it has had no more political or institutional connection than any ordinary American town has with its local industrial interests. The Corporation has by no means paid more than its share of the local taxes, and the schools, in particular, have not only been quite free from the Corporation influence or support, but have even at times run so far counter to the approval of the Corporation officials that the school administration has had difficulty in acquiring its needed sites for new schools. It can be emphatically said that the schools of Gary are no more the product of peculiar conditions than are the schools of numberless rapidly growing Western towns.

The mushroom growth of Gary has not meant a peculiar kind of a town, but simply the telescoping into a few years of the typical municipal evils of graft, franchise fights, saloon dominance, insufficient housing and health regulation, election frauds, and lack of social cohesion. Its dramatic growth has not prevented its becoming a very typical American city. In April, 1906, Gary was a waste of sand-dunes and scrub-oak swamps at the southern end of Lake Michigan. Three years later it had a steel plant covering an area of a square mile and capable of employing 140,000 men; it had a population of 12,000; 15 miles of paved streets, 25 miles of cement sidewalks, $2,000,000 worth of residences, sewer, water, gas, and electric facilities; it had 2 banks, 6 hotels, 3 dailies, 2 schools, 10 church denominations, 46 lawyers, 24 physicians — in short, all the paraphernalia of the modern city. The visitor who goes to-day to Gary finds a typically varied American city, rather better built than the average, and rather unusually favored in its open spaces. Situated within thirty miles of Chicago, the city presents a rather pleasing contrast to the long chain of industrial towns that stretches for miles in every direction across the treeless prairie. With a well-built business section, lines of residence streets, handsome public buildings and churches, electric cars and taxicabs, Gary has a settled air of community life unusual even for an older town. It has almost the aspect of a commercial rather than an industrial center. It is the focus of the county trade, and the extent of its business and middle-class residential districts is somewhat larger than in neighboring towns. The steel mills and subsidiary plants are massed along the lake and the artificially constructed harbor. The great immigrant population, largely of cheap and illiterate proletarian labor from southeastern Europe, inhabits the congested district of the South Side. The mills are separated from the town by a small river which forms almost a moat for the great industrial fortress. The town is laid out in checkerboard fashion, with a wide main avenue a hundred feet wide and cross-streets sixty feet wide. Alleys run the long way of the blocks, and contain the sewer and water mains. Ethnologically the population is very mixed. Thirty nationalities are said to be represented in the schools, but this large foreign population is a familiar phenomenon in the American industrial town. A rough census taken in 1908 gave the foreign population of Gary as fifty-six per cent of the whole. In 1912 it was only forty per cent, or a decrease of sixteen per cent. The alien influx has not destroyed the essentially characteristic American features of the city. The native American element has always predominated politically and socially. For an American city of its size to-day, Gary represents, not a specialized community, but a fairly harmonious distribution of social classes, races, occupations, and interests. It is essentially a normal, variedly functioning, independent community, and the schools have been developed to meet the needs of a modern varied urban community.

It must be emphasized that neither the demands of a peculiar type of industrial community nor the work of benevolent philanthropy created the schools of Gary. They have been developed in response to the typically current needs of a normal American municipality. They have had to meet the same situations which all American cities are confronting in their effort to educate "all the children of all the people."

Organized under a school administration consisting of a board of education with three members working in conjunction with a superintendent of schools, the school system depends for support entirely upon local taxation and the usual sources of revenue, and enjoys no unusual municipal or financial advantages. On the contrary, the enterprise of providing public schools for the town of Gary was one of peculiar difficulty. The new and rapidly growing town required the immediate creation of a school plant, in addition to the annual cost of instruction and maintenance.

The community was poor. A large proportion of the people, being recently arrived immigrants, owned no taxable property. The plants of the Steel Corporation, the most valuable property in the community, were habitually undervalued in the assessments. The state laws, moreover, provide that school revenues for any given year are to be obtained on an assessment made almost two years before. The result in a new city like Gary, where the population had been doubling each year, was, therefore, that current school revenues had to be based on assessment values obtained when the population was only one quarter as great.

In the face of all these formidable difficulties the success of the Gary school system seems little short of amazing. In the short space of eight years the population has increased from three hundred to over thirty thousand. No ordinary city would attempt to supply school facilities to a population which doubled every year. The mere physical problem of providing seats for the children would be insurmountable. A city which followed the conventional school plan would be swamped. At the present time, with their much slower yearly increase of population, half of the cities of over one hundred thousand in this country have insufficient sittings for their children.

Yet with its leaping movement of population the city of Gary has been able to provide not only full-time instruction for every child, but actually a longer school day. It has not only done this, but it has provided evening-school instruction for an even greater number of adults. There is something pardonable in the Gary boast that every third person in the city goes to school. And Gary has succeeded not only in giving this universal schooling, but in making it what is probably the most varied and stimulating elementary public-school instruction in the United States, with an equipment in buildings and facilities for work, study, and play which is surpassed, if anywhere, only in specially favored communities. All this has been done with a normal tax-rate, and at a *per-capita* cost of both construction and maintenance no greater than that in the city of Chicago and the city of New York, with their many overcrowded and poorly equipped school-buildings. The Gary schools, at the same time, have paid the highest teachers' salaries in the State. The entire achievement has been as brilliant as the difficulties confronted were formidable.

It is these remarkable results that have focused the attention of so many educators on Gary, and it will be the purpose of this book to expound the "unique and ingenious synthesis of educational influences" which has made them possible. If, then, in the course of eight years, the schools of Gary have acquired a wide reputation as a momentous educational experiment which has passed into successful demonstration, the fact must be laid entirely to the abilities of the school authorities, and not to any adventitious factors of the community situation or of private assistance. The dominating factor was the personal genius of the superintendent, William Wirt, who was called to Gary in 1908 from Bluffton, Indiana, where he had been in charge of the public schools, and where he had partly worked out some of the ideas which he was later to develop so comprehensively in the Gary schools. When it is objected that the

Gary plan is an experiment, and that eight years are scarcely sufficient time to pronounce upon its merits, it must be remembered that the real experimental stage of the Gary plan consisted in the eight years in Bluffton. Mr. Wirt came to Gary with his educational ideas matured after this long testing. He was brought to Gary by the unusually progressive mayor and school board of the new town, for the express purpose of working out on a large scale the principles which they had seen in concrete application at Bluffton. Against the financial meagerness of the town's resources and the obstructiveness of the founders must, therefore, be set the advantage of having a virgin field in which to work. The superintendent and school board were able in a remarkably short time to build up a public interest and support which has been a very large asset. The people of Gary seem proud of their schools, and seem to appreciate the comprehensive educational and recreational facilities which through them are provided for both children and adults. Few educational experiments have been so successful in technique and in popular support. The Gary schools represent the fruit of a very unusual combination of educational philosophy, economic engineering, and political sagacity. Circumstances seem to have conspired to produce a school system which unites a very remarkable school plant with a synthesis of novel plans of operation which are fertile in suggestion to school men, if they do not tend to revolutionize many methods of financing public schools as well as methods of administration and teaching.

This outline of the setting of the Gary schools scarcely puts the background in its correct light. When we speak of the "Gary school" we are really talking about something bigger than the educational system of a small Western city. What we have to deal with is an educational idea, a comprehensive plan for the modern public school, capable of general imitation and adaptation to the needs of other American communities. In this sense it means primarily what Superintendent Wirt thought a public school should be. Being at once a social engineer and educational philosopher, he has succeeded in working out a type-plan of public school which to many educators appears uniquely valuable in American public education. The discussion which follows attempts to describe the Gary schools from this larger point of view. The effort is to show in detail how the plan actually works in the schools of Gary, while at the same time to suggest the larger ideas and principles which have motivated it. The "Gary plan" represents, of course, not only what has been done in Gary, but its further implications and tendencies, as well as the developments and modifications now working out in those schools, such as the group in New York City, which have been put in the hands of the Gary authorities for reorganization.

II

THE SCHOOL PLANT: EDUCATING THE WHOLE CHILD

This children's community, as worked out by Mr. Wirt in the Gary schools, is a work-study-and-play school of the most varied kind. It represents, in fact, an ideal school plant which was well outlined in Mr. Wirt's mind when he first came to Gary. Schools like the magnificent Emerson and Froebel plants in Gary, and the new Pestalozzi School, for which plans have already been drawn and the site bought, represent the working-out in concrete form of this ideal. At the same time, it must be understood that the essential features of the Wirt plan are possible in schools which were not built from the ideal plan. Perhaps Mr. Wirt's greatest triumph in Gary is not these new schools, but the old Jefferson School, which he found when he came to the town, and which, by ingenious remodeling, he turned from a conventional school-building into a completely functioning school. If the

Wirt plan is momentous as showing what a really modern public school should embody, it is no less momentous in showing how easily the old type of schoolhouse may be adapted to the varied life of the school community that is the Wirt school.

It will first be necessary to describe the ideal school plant as represented in the Emerson and Froebel Schools in Gary. This plant carries out a belief in educating the whole child, physically, artistically, manually, scientifically, as well as intellectually. Mr. Wirt believes that by putting in the child's way all the opportunities for varied development, the child will be able to select those activities for which he is best suited, and thus develop his capacities to their highest power. This can be done only in a school which provides, besides the ordinary classrooms, also playgrounds and gardens, gymnasiums and swimming-pools, special drawing and music studios, science laboratories, machine shops, and intimate and constant contact with supplementary community activities outside the school. The Wirt school is based on a fourfold unity of interests, — play and exercise, intellectual

THE EMERSON SCHOOL

study, special work in shop and laboratory, etc., and social and expressive activity in auditorium or outside community agency.

Between these activities there is no invidious distinction. The manual and artistic are not subordinated to the intellectual, as in the ordinary school. The "special activities" are not mere trimmings to the "regular work," but neither is the latter neglected in favor of the former. The ideal of the Wirt plan is that the child should have every day, in some form or other, contact with all the different activities which influence a well-rounded human being, instead of meeting them perfunctorily once or twice a week, as in the ordinary school. This does not mean, of course, that every child is expected to develop into a versatile genius, equally able in science and music and shopwork and history. Most children are sternly limited in their capacities, and will be unable to assimilate more than a small part of what the school offers them. But the Wirt school definitely offers the opportunity. If there are capacities, they have the chance to develop, while no child need lack that speaking acquaintance with the varied interests of work and study which now the old traditional type of school so tragically denies.

It is an essential feature of the Wirt scheme that this varied work be provided for all the children from the earliest possible years. The lavish equipment of the ideal Wirt school plant may be paralleled in other communities than Gary, but it is paralleled only in the case of the secondary schools. It is a notorious fact that, of the children who begin the American public school, only one fifth ever reach even the first year of the high school. So far it is the high school or the highest grammar grades that have received practically all of the advantages of broadening educational endeavor, — vocational training, science laboratory work, the study of civics, domestic science, etc. This means that the vast majority of school-children leave school with nothing but the barest intellectual training, without ever having come in contact with points of view and ways of doing things that are absolutely essential to any understanding or effectiveness in the world above the very lowest. Against this fundamentally undemocratic system, which denies help to those who need it most, the Wirt plan resolutely sets its face.

The ideal Wirt school contains in one school plant the complete school, with all the classes from the kindergarten through the common school and high school.

By this plan both economic and educational advantages are realized. From an economic point of view, it is cheaper to have large, completely equipped centers than to duplicate the equipment in a number of smaller centers. From an educational point of view, it enables pupils to bridge the chasm between the elementary grades and the high school. By ceasing to make the high school a separate institution to be "entered" or "graduated from," pupils find no place to stop when they have completed the eight grades.

The complete school, Mr. Wirt believes, offers important moral gains. "The development of character, habits of industry, reliability, good health, and the growth of intelligence require time," he says, "and must be a continuous process throughout the entire life of the child." The complete school gives an opportunity for that coöperation or "apprenticeship" between the younger and older children, which is so important a feature of the Wirt school, and this association breaks down the snobbery of age which causes so much unhappiness in childhood.

It must be admitted that in Gary, owing to the progressive mortality in attendance which is common everywhere, it is possible to realize the complete school only in the Emerson and Froebel plants. At the same time it must be remembered that these schools care for three quarters of the school-children of the town. In the elementary schools which Mr. Wirt is reorganizing in New York, he is asking that there shall be included at least two of the high-school years, in order that the complete school may be approximated as closely as possible. In Gary, they are working for a school which is even more than "complete," for they aim to include even the first year and perhaps even the second of the ordinary college course. Stretching down boldly past the kindergarten to a nursery for babies, and up into the college itself, the Wirt school thus gives a fundamentally new orientation to education, shows it graphically and practically as a continuous process, and breaks down those artificial barriers by which we measure off "education," and make it easy for people to "finish" it. The Wirt school seems definitely to forecast the day when the public school will have swallowed the college, and the "higher education" will have become as local and available as the three R's.

If the school is to educate the whole child, the first need is evidently a place for him to grow. "The best of education," says Professor Terman, "is but wisely directed growth." "The activities of a child," says Professor Dewey, "are the means by which he becomes acquainted with his world, and by which he learns the use and limits of his own powers." The lack of free activity in the conventional school has been the major cause of those symptoms of morbidity which school hygienists have brought to the attention of educators within the last few years. Over-pressure and confinement have made the school a manufactory for evils which the next generation will look back to with amazement at the blindness of the educational world which permitted it.

The ideal school will make the playground the very center of its life. The school in the Wirt plan covers a site of from ten to twenty acres. Actually the Emerson School in Gary has ten acres; Froebel has twelve; the new Tolleston site covers twenty acres. Of this ideal site of twenty acres, ten acres in front of the school-building are purchased by the city and maintained by it as an open public square or small park. The remaining ten acres are bought by the school for the building site and playgrounds. It is the intention in Gary to have these park-school playgrounds distributed over the city so that few families will live more than half a mile away from one of them.

It is a cardinal principle of the Wirt plan that the parks and playgrounds of a city should be placed as *adjuncts of the schools*. It is the schools that they primarily serve and it is with the schools that they should be grouped. Millions of dollars have been wasted in the public-playground movement in this country through disregard of this fact. There is a good story of a Chicago playground instructor who, when asked if the playgrounds coöperated with the schools, replied, "Sure we do! If we see any kid on here between nine and three, we chase him off!" This is symbolic of the lack of intelligent coöperation between child-welfare agencies. It is this wasteful and ineffective situation which the Wirt plan remedies by boldly annexing park and playground to the school itself. A comparison of the Chicago playgrounds with the Gary school playgrounds shows the immensely greater public service rendered under the Wirt scheme. Chicago has one of the most elaborate systems of recreation parks and field-houses in the country. Yet in a district only *one fortieth* the size of the Chicago district, one Gary school, providing for both children and adults, gave indoor gymnasium work to three times as many people; shower-baths to one third as many; outdoor gymnasium to an equal number; the use of swimming-pools to half as many; use of the assembly halls to four times as many; and to as many, the use of clubrooms and reading-rooms. Thus, in educating the child's body, and giving him space to grow and play, the Wirt school enormously increased the opportunities of every one in the district, old and young, to secure the same advantages.

The ideal Wirt school plant, such as the Emerson School in Gary, in its open space of ten acres, besides its playground filled with apparatus, has gardens, tennis courts, ball fields, running tracks, and handball courts. For the younger children there are wading-pools and sandpits. One field is arranged so that it may be flooded in winter for skating. There are two acres of school-gardens, and a cluster of cages and houses for the animals of the school zoo. The outdoor equipment is, in other words, on the scale of a college or a wealthy private school which can afford spacious grounds and provision for every athletic sport. The Gary schools are, however, public schools, and these facilities are open to all the children of all ages and all the time.

It is customary for our newer high schools to have gymnasiums, but the common school is rarely provided for. In the Wirt school, the common school shares, of course, in the extensive gymnasium equipment. The Emerson School has two gymnasiums, one for boys and one for girls. It has also a large swimming-

THE SWIMMING-POOL AT THE FROEBEL SCHOOL

pool. The Froebel School has two gymnasiums and two swimming-pools. The Jefferson School has a large gymnasium, though only the common school is provided for in the Jefferson. The other Gary schools all have gymnasiums proportionate to their size. In the new school plants it is intended to build pergolas about the inner court which will contain open-air classrooms and additional outdoor gymnasium space. Nothing is omitted which will provide the right physical conditions for the child's growth and development from his earliest years.

Coming to the school building itself, we find in the Emerson and Froebel Schools architectural creations of unusual beauty and impressiveness. The school building is built around a great court, with broad halls as wide as streets, and well lighted from the court. These broad halls serve not only as the school streets for the constant passage of the children between their work, but also as centers for the "application" work, or for informal study. They are so wide that all confusion is avoided, and they suggest to the visitor that they serve the school community in the same way that the agora or forum did the ancient city. In the Emerson School the beginning of an art gallery has been made. It suggests the idea that just as the schools ought to absorb the playgrounds, so they ought to absorb the museums and galleries. Pictures and objects of art and interest become unreal and artificial when immured in isolated museums, which can be visited only at special times and with effort. They should be at hand in the school, fertilizing and beautifying every moment of its daily life. The artistic sense can be cultivated only by bringing children into contact daily and almost unconsciously with beautiful things. The schools themselves must be art galleries, and these fine corridors of the Wirt school indicate the way by which a wholly new orientation is to be given to our public galleries by using them as adjuncts to the education of children.

Similarly with museums. The teaching of the Gary schools, based fundamentally on concrete things and processes, needs to be constantly in touch with the objects which it is our custom to store in dead museums. The school museum is an essential feature of the

Wirt school. The Wirt plan does not contemplate the taking of children docilely about to visit museums, as some progressive teachers are doing. It contemplates bringing the museums into the schools, so that the children can know the treasures and live with them and learn about them.

And similarly with libraries. Mr. Wirt believes that the school may do the work of the public library much more efficiently and much more economically than the library can itself do it. He has shown in Gary that in a school branch of the public library, library maintenance and circulation cost per book circulation is only about five per cent of the cost in the main library, while the life of the book circulated in sets under the control of the teachers is ten times that of the usual circulation book in the library. In both the Emerson and Froebel Schools there is a branch of the public library, under a library assistant. Children use the library as a part of their regular work under the supervision of the assistant and teachers. All sorts of stereoscopic pictures, photographs, collections of pictures, atlases, etc., can thus be provided, which would be impossible for the classroom. The library becomes the storehouse of the knowledge of the school, and the children learn to recognize it as such. Again, the library is already an important feature of many of the newer high schools throughout the country. In the Wirt school, however, all the elementary classes use it also.

The Wirt school contemplates bringing all the cultural resources of the community to bear on the school. It makes the school the proper and natural depository for whatever the community has to offer in artistic interest or intellectual resource. Like most of the features of the Wirt plan, this consolidation of gallery, museum, and library in the school is as economically efficient as it is educationally valuable.

A word must be said about the auditorium. Few schools have assembly rooms like that in the Froebel School in Gary, with its stage large enough for a full-sized basketball game or athletic contest. The unique rôle of the auditorium in the Wirt school will be described in the next chapter. It assists materially in educating the whole child by giving him opportunities for public expression before the school community.

The classrooms in the ideal Wirt school are much more attractive than the ordinary classrooms, far less formal and far less crowded. In some of them the old-fashioned school desk and seat have been retained, largely, according to Mr. Wirt, to meet the prejudice of the parents. Owing to the frequent change and movement of classes, however, this peculiarly flagrant instrument of educational perversity does little harm. Many of the lower grades have a desk, made in the school, which is a kind of workbench. These desks have vises attached, and loose tops, which can be readily replaced when soiled or worn out. The seat is a four-legged stool, which can be pushed out of the way when the child is using his desk for a workbench. On occasion the children can take up their stools and desktops and go off to work in the halls or garden. Such a room is an ideal classroom, with its hint of the workshop and its lack of rigidity. In the history room in the Emerson School are broad tables that can be used for map-drawing. The idea is to give to each classroom the physical setting and the furniture which will best enable a particular kind of work to be done there. The result is that the classrooms of the Wirt schools have a character of their own, quite different from the colorless and depressing effect of the ordinary classroom. They are not merely rooms where children study together and tamely recite, but essentially workshops where children do interesting things with their minds, just as in the shops they do interesting things with their hands. The history room is a real history laboratory. Maps and charts made by the pupils cover the walls, magazines lie about, pictures and books overflow the tables. The visitor realizes that he is in a room saturated with history, past and present. It is easier to learn in a room where everything appeals to the imagination.

Mr. Wirt says that you never can tell when a child is learning. The time that he makes progress is not necessarily the recitation time. It is the constant impingement of impressions that really educates him, and it is this that the intellectual side of the Wirt school is skillfully designed to cultivate. Music and expression and drawing are taught, not in regular classrooms, but in special studios, which are genuine studios equipped with all the facilities to impress upon the child with what seriousness these things are taken in the Wirt school. Art tends to mean much more to a child brought up in such a school, because he works at it in an impressive environment.

The science laboratories for botany, zoölogy, chemistry, physics, are not only well-equipped laboratories, but workshops as well. The botany room in the Gary school has a large conservatory of vines and plants at the end; the zoölogy room has a menagerie of small pets, fowls and birds, guinea-pigs and rabbits. The physics rooms are in contact with a machine room where automobiles and other machines illustrate the practical application of scientific principles. Everywhere the attempt is made to give a dramatic and practical physical setting to the work and study, so that the child may be learning all the time by suggestion and imitation. And everywhere the attempt is made to show that no one activity is any more important than any other. Each activity represents one side of that whole child to educate whom this school plant has been built.

The manual and industrial work is, of course, an essential feature of the Wirt school. The shops are much more extensive than is customary in even the most progressive public school, or even in the special trade school. The Emerson School in Gary has, for instance, a carpentry-shop, cabinet-shop, paint-shop, foundry, forge, machine-shop, printery, sheet-metal shop, electrical shop, sewing-room, and cooking- and dining-rooms, all admirably equipped as regular shops, and not merely as manual-training rooms. The Froebel School has, besides these shops, a plumbing-shop, a laundry, a shoemaking-shop and a pottery-shop. In the smaller schools several shops are combined into one, as at the Jefferson, though the work done is just as genuine as at the ideal plant. The number of shops, or the variety of work, is, as we shall see in the next chapter, limited only by the services which the school demands in the way of repairing or enhancing its physical facilities.

When we have mentioned the room for commercial studies, the supply-store, the kindergartens and nurseries, the draughting-rooms, indoor playrooms, teachers' room, conservatory, doctor's room and dental clinic, offices, etc., our survey of the school plant is complete. The arrangement of rooms itself, however, is very significant. As we pass around the second floor of the Froebel School, for instance, we meet, in this order, pottery-shop, laundry, freehand drawing-room, two classrooms, physics laboratory, music and expression studios, conservatory, two classrooms, botany laboratory, and four more classrooms. The shops are not segregated in the basement, but the children in their various activities work side by side. Classrooms are placed next to laboratories, and shops next to studios, in order to impress the pupil with the unity of the program, and in order that the younger pupils may have constantly before their eyes an inviting future and opportunity. All the rooms, moreover, have glass doors, and the shops have windows, so that the children, passing through the halls, may look in and see others at work at unfamiliar tasks. In this way their curiosity is likely to be aroused and the ambition to work at these interesting activities in which they see the older children engaged.

In this juxtaposition of the various activities, therefore, the child has impressed upon him that school life is a unity in breadth, just as the combining of the elementary and secondary school impresses him with the fact that his school life is a unity in length. No opportunity is lost to touch his imagination and excite his curiosity. The school plant itself, in its mere arrangement and construction, it will thus be seen, serves a very important educational purpose. The careful detail with which this has been worked out in these ideal school plants of Gary makes the Wirt school in its physical aspect something very much more significant than a mere collection of facilities. Those facilities fit into one another according to a very comprehensive plan. They form organs of a genuine school life, which educates the whole child.

This fourfold division of study and recitation facilities, studio, workshop, and laboratory facilities, auditorium facilities, and application and play facilities, is essential to the working of the Wirt plan. Where the ideal school plant is impossible, this fourfold plan may yet be possible. As has been said, the greatest triumph of the Wirt plan in Gary is, perhaps, the Jefferson School, a building of conventional style, which had been erected before Mr. Wirt came to Gary. It was an ordinary school building with ten classrooms and auditorium, but no other facilities. By turning the spacious attic into a gymnasium, by transforming five of the classrooms into music and art studios and nature-study laboratories, by building a general jack-of-all-trades workshop around the engine- and boiler-room in the cellar, by building a domestic-science kitchen in an unused corner, putting lockers into wasted space, and by equipping the playground with apparatus, Mr. Wirt succeeded in transforming an ordinary school building, whose prototype may be found in almost any town in the land, into a full-fledged, varied, and smoothly running Wirt school. The reorganization of schools in New York City and other places has been done by Mr. Wirt along similar lines.[1]

[1] See appendix for detailed description of reorganization of twelve New York schools.

Where, in most cases, a mere rearrangement of classrooms and the institution of shops and laboratories will transform a school, in others special annexes are necessary. These can be built usually, however, at comparatively small cost. The use of portable houses by the smaller schools of Gary has enabled the small wayside "district school," hitherto confined entirely to study and recitation, to transform itself into a genuine Wirt school, with its fourfold work and study. Shop, auditorium, and laboratory and studio can be provided in the form of small portable houses, and the capacity of the school as well as its facilities can thus be greatly increased.

III

WORK, STUDY, AND PLAY: THE SCHOOL AS A COMMUNITY

THE Gary school represents not merely the old public school with certain added modern features, but a definite reorganization. Its aim is to form, with its well-balanced facilities of work, study, and play, a genuine children's community, where the children's normal healthy interests are centered, and where they learn, in Professor Dewey's phrase, "by doing the things that have meaning to them as children." The Gary school aims to meet the comparative failure of the public school to-day to care for the city child. It tries to take the place of the old household and rural community life which provided for our forefathers the practical education of which the city child in his daily life is deprived to-day.

The full significance of the Gary plan can scarcely be understood unless it is seen against this background. "It is impossible," says Professor Dewey, "to exaggerate the amount of mental and moral training secured by our forefathers in the course of the ordinary pursuits of life. They were engaged in subduing a new country. Industry was at a premium, and instead of being of a routine nature pioneer conditions required initiative, ingenuity, and pluck. . . . Production had not yet been concentrated in factories in congested centers, but was distributed through villages. . . . The occupations of daily life engaged the imagination and enforced knowledge of natural materials and processes. . . . Children had the discipline that came from sharing in useful activities. . . . Under such conditions the schools could hardly have done better than devote themselves to books. . . . But conditions changed, and school materials and methods did not change to keep pace. Population shifted to urban centers. Production became a mass affair carried on in big factories, instead of a household affair. . . . Industry was no longer a local or neighborhood concern. Manufacturing was split up into a very great variety of separate processes through the economies incident upon extreme division of labor. . . . The machine worker, unlike the older hand worker, is following blindly the intelligence of others instead of his own knowledge of materials, tools and processes. . . . Children have lost the moral and practical discipline that once came from sharing in the round of home duties. For a large number there is little alternative, especially in large cities, between irksome child labor and demoralizing child idleness."

The Gary school is an organized attempt to restore this natural education, adapt it to modern demands, and thus avoid these alternatives so disastrous for the future of the child and the quality of the coming generation. By making the public school as much as possible a self-sustaining child community, Superintendent Wirt believes that all the benefits of this older education can be attained. "We cannot," he says, "trust the other social institutions to remedy the defects. Not more than one quarter of the urban children attend Sunday-School regularly. This makes an average of only two minutes a day for all the days and all the children. In fact, church, Sunday-School, public library, public playgrounds, Y.M.C.A., Boy Scouts, and all other child-welfare agencies do not occupy the time of all the children of a city for more than an average of ten minutes a day. The practical effect of this is that the streets and alleys and the cheap theaters and other commercialized places of amusement have the children for over five hours a day. The cities are not fit places for the rearing of children, because, as a rule, the streets and alleys have twice the time for educating the children in the wrong direction that the school, church, library, and playground have for educating them in the right direction."

This is the justification for extending the Gary school day to eight hours and limiting vacations. This is the plan which gives ample time for the intensive use of the remarkable school plant described in the preceding chapter. For in place of using for the special work and play activities a part of the already too few regular school hours per year, the Gary school secures additional time for these activities by appropriating the now worse than wasted "street and alley time" of the masses of city children. Saturday school, vacation school, even an all-year school, are features of the Gary plan which carry out this principle of providing a school life for the children for as long a time as they can be induced and encouraged to continue it. The Gary school deliberately seeks to employ and satisfy the children's time with wholesome and interesting activity.

It aims not only to organize the daily life of the child for the greater part of his time, but it seeks to provide for him in a self-sustaining community. This means that all the work and study converge upon the school life. The things that are done in the Gary school contribute to the usefulness, the beauty, or the interest of the school community. The Gary school is built on the sound psychological theory that only such work as has meaning in the life of the school, as lived by the children themselves then and there, will be really learned and assimilated. The school is not only to be a "preparation for life": it is to be a life itself, as the old household was a life itself. "The idea that children should study exclusively for eight years, and then work exclusively for the rest of their life," says Superintendent Wirt, "is really a new idea in civilization. The criticism of the modern public school is directed almost entirely at the helplessness of children who are attempting to enter industrial and commercial life from this exclusive study period of eight, twelve, or sixteen years in the schools, and at the fact that the school is not able to get more than half its children beyond the sixth grade of the common school. Formerly the school plus the home and small shop educated the child. The small shop has been generally eliminated and the home has lost most of its former opportunities. A much greater part of the education of the child must be assumed by the school of the present generation. In place of the school, home, and shop, we have the school and the city street educating the great masses of children. The school must do what the school, home, and small shop formerly did together."

The idea of making the school a self-sustaining community is worked out in the Gary school in the most comprehensive form. The manual-training and industrial shops, for instance, are actually the shops for the school community, and their work goes largely toward the upkeep of the school plant. Vocational training in the Gary school means that whatever work is necessary in the way of repairing, conserving, beautifying, or enhancing the school facilities is done by the pupils themselves. The school, like the old-time industrial home and community, has a large amount of real work that is now being done and must always be done in connection with the equipment of its buildings, grounds, laboratories, shops, etc. The large, lavishly equipped Gary school plants require a force of mechanics to keep them in repair. The usual way of doing this would be to hire outside labor at considerable expense to do the necessary work during school vacations. The Gary schools, on the other hand, which have no long vacations, employ a permanent force of mechanics, and keep them continuously employed throughout the year. Regular union artisans, chosen because of their character, intelligence, and teaching ability, are engaged by the building departments of the school plant. There are carpenters, cabinet-makers, painters, plumbers, sheet-metal workers, engineers, printers, electricians, machinists, foundrymen, etc., sufficient to meet the needs of the schools. This great variety of equipment and maintenance work provides manual activity of a truly educative sort suitable to every stage of the child's development. The shops of these workmen become the regular manual and industrial training shops of the school. The children work with the artisans in much the same way as old-time apprentices, though, of course, for only a fraction of their time. Just as the child formerly participated in the industrial activities of the household, so now he participates in the real industrial activities of his school. The school artisans, and the nurses, school dentist, and physician, landscape gardener, architect, and draftsman, accountant, storekeeper, office force, lunch-room manager, designer, dressmaker, milliner, all take the place of the father and mother and older brothers and sisters in the old-time, self-sustaining, practically educative household. The children receive all the benefits of doing real work that must be done and of participating in their own school business. And they have the benefit of a completely modern equipment resembling in detail the machinery and processes which they will find when they go out into the larger social community.

In this novel scheme the Gary schools seem to have experienced little difficulty. Superintendent Wirt says that when you have provided a plant where the children may live a complete life eight hours a day in work, study, and play, it is the simplest thing imaginable to permit the children in the workshops, under the direction and with the help of well-trained men and women, to assume the responsibility for the maintenance of the school plant. There can be no exploitation of the children, for masters and pupils are permitted to do only enough work to balance the wages of the masters and the cost of materials. The teacher-workmen would be doing the work whether the children assisted or not. They earn their salaries by their repair and construction work, and the children who desire it get an admirably practical vocational training almost without additional cost to the city. The great expense is avoided of special shop equipment, such as the usual industrial high school or special trade school has for its industrial courses, which are, moreover, wholly unproductive. And the school is able to offer a much greater variety of trades than even the special trade school: for a school plant like the Gary institution will demand for its equipment and maintenance almost every staple trade, industrial and domestic, with the attendant educational opportunities for both boy and girl.

Manual work takes on quite a new meaning when it becomes, as in the Gary schools, productive work for the school community. It is no longer a question of each child doing his "practice" work, his stereotyped "stunt," in which he soon loses interest. The boys in the Gary carpenter-shop are making desks and tables for the classrooms, cabinets and stools for the laboratories, or bookracks for the library. In the paint-shop they are staining and finishing them; or they are at work on the woodwork of the building, painting or varnishing. The electricians must care for motors, bells, etc., and there is always opportunity for teaching winding, motor construction, and wiring. Plumbing must be installed and kept in repair. Many parts of the plant call for the sheet-metal worker. Foundry and machine workers require in turn a pattern-making shop and draftsmen to furnish plans and specifications. The engineer of the heating, lighting, and ventilating plant gives lessons in firing and in the care of boilers. The printing-shop does all the printing work for the schools, — blanks, forms, reports, charts, etc., besides the illustrated brochures which the pupils of the various departments issue. In the Froebel School there is even a demand for a pottery shop, where the children often discover artistic talent in making the necessary clay utensils for the school. The number and character of the school shops is limited only by the needs of the school community. One year the shoeless condition of some of the children set a demand for a shoe shop, in which old shoes were made over into wearable new ones.

The visitor to the Gary school finds everywhere little groups of busy children, absorbedly interested, working on the different needs of the school, under kindly and intelligent teacher-workmen. He finds that there is enough real work in the school plant to keep occupied for his hour or more a day every child who is interested in manual work — and most children are — or who desires to become familiar with a trade. Such work is highly educational, and it is not drudgery. It is not specialized, nor is it segregated from the academic studies. The industrial work for both boys and girls is an integral part of the school life in which every one who cares for a rounded education must participate in some form or other.

There is not a department which does not contribute in some way to the school community life. The caretakers of the grounds are under the supervision of the botany and zoölogy (nature study) departments. The children work with them in taking charge of and caring for the gardens, lawns, trees, and shrubs. The botany classes care also for the school conservatory and for the smaller experimental conservatory in the botany laboratory. The zoölogy classes have charge of the school zoo as well as the collection of pets in the zoölogy room. Even the drawing classes contribute, the mechanical-drawing pupils in preparing plans for the industrial work and construction, the art classes in decorating the

THE PRINTING SHOP AT THE EMERSON SCHOOL

friezes of their room or in designing details for the building.

Domestic science in the Gary school is not taught as a separate "subject." It means the practical operation of the school lunch-room under the direction of an instructor and a cook assistant. The domestic-science room is a real kitchen, dining-room, and pantry in which the daily lunch is prepared and served to such teachers and pupils as desire it. The domestic-science work for the girls then consists of nothing but this daily service, older and younger girls coöperating with cook and teacher. The salary of the assistant is paid out of the profits of the lunch-room. Since the food is sold, all expenses for supplies are charged to the lunch department. The sewing-room is operated on a similar plan. The instructor has as assistants a practical dressmaker, laundress, and milliner. Their salaries and all materials used are paid for from the savings made by doing the necessary laundry and needlework for the school. Both cooking and sewing departments are therefore *self-sustaining school-community shops*. The school board makes no appropriations for the support of the lunch-room, dressmaking, laundry, and millinery departments other than the salaries of the two head teachers. All bills are paid directly by the department managers, and no accounts are kept by the school board. The other shops are self-supporting in the sense that the ordinary appropriations for painting, cabinet-work, electrical work, plumbing, printing, etc. (which would have to be paid anyway), generally pay the salaries of the teacher-workmen and the costs of the material. The ideal attainment would be to make the shops all self-sustaining school-community shops.

The work of all these shops requires elaborate systems of accounting. All this work is taken charge of by the instructors and pupils of the commercial departments of the school. The work the children do in the shops is computed on the basis of regular union wages for the particular trade, and they are "paid" in imitation checks, upon which their standing in the course is based. For these payments the commercial pupils manage a regular school banking system, with savings accounts, etc. They also have charge, under the instructors' supervision, of all the regular accounting and secretarial work for the school administration. Thus their bookkeeping, stenography, and typewriting contribute directly to the needs of the school. The commercial pupils also take care of the ordering and distribution of supplies. Some of these, such as the coal and cement used in the schools, are in turn tested by the chemistry classes in their laboratory to see whether they come up to specifications. The school "store" is as important a feature of the school community as the school "bank," and the commercial pupils take turns in "keeping" it. The criticism that the pupils are incompetent to handle all these matters is met by the obvious consideration that the school cannot afford to graduate pupils in accounting and secretarial work who cannot perform these functions efficiently for themselves and their school. At present, it should be mentioned, these departments are said not to be self-supporting, in the way that the domestic-science shops are.

If the school is to be the children's community, there must be some place of general assembly, some forum or theater where the school may take stock of itself. This is provided in the "auditorium," one of the original and essential features of the Gary plan. "Auditorium," to which a daily hour is given, is devoted to purposes different from the religious exercises, declamations, and moral homilies common to the "opening exercises" of the ordinary school. It does not even open the day, for the Gary program makes it necessary for the "auditorium" hour to come at periods throughout the day, differing for different classes. The aim is to make it an occasion where anything that is happening of peculiar interest in any part of the school may be dramatically brought to the attention of the rest of the school. In the Gary school, each child goes to "auditorium" for a full hour each day, and listens to a program contributed by pupils or teachers or outside visitors. There is always choral singing; there may be instrumental or phonograph music besides. Lantern-slides and motion-pictures are often shown. There may be talks by the special teachers about their work. The child may see there gymnastic exhibitions, — as has been said, the stage at the Froebel School is so large that a full-sized basketball game may be played upon it before the audience, — folk-dancing, or dramatic dialogues and little plays written by the pupils themselves about interesting things in their study or reading. There may be debates on school issues. What is to be presented in "auditorium" is limited only by the imagination and expressiveness of teachers and children. The teachers in turn have the responsibility of arranging the program, in coöperation with their pupils. Children of widely different ages are sent together to the "auditorium" hour, so that the younger may have their curiosity stimulated about the work of classes that they perhaps have not yet reached, and so that the older may lose that snobbery of age which often causes so much unhappiness in childhood, and tends to fill the adult mind with delusions about the young. This plan, therefore, makes for sympathy between the pupils, makes each child familiar with the activities of the whole school, and prevents that unfortunate segregation and confinement of the ordinary school. Besides being able to look into the various rooms through the glass doors, the child in the Gary school has an opportunity of seeing in "auditorium" in dramatic form the life of his school. The influence of this "auditorium" hour upon the school work, particularly the academic work, can hardly fail to be marked, for it directly motivates all the studies. It is a sort of communal "application" activity. History and literature take on a new meaning, because the material may be studied now always in the light of its possible presentation to the rest of the school in dramatic and intelligent form. Many schools use the dramatic sense to vitalize these studies, but no other school provides so definite and regular a focus, and so constant and interested an audience for the products of such a vitalization. The "auditorium" in the Gary school seems to be a genuine school-community theater, an inevitable and integral part of the school life.

In the words of Superintendent Wirt, the Gary school aims to be a "clearing-house for children's activities." The ideal is to render the school community as self-sustaining and self-stimulating as possible. Whatever the school cannot itself contribute to the education of the child, it may find in the institutions of the surrounding community. Any outside agency which provides wholesome activities for children becomes then a sort of extension of the school. Children in the Gary school are permitted to go out from their play or "auditorium" hour to do special work at home, take private music or art lessons, visit the Y.M.C.A., settlement or neighborhood house, attend the Boy Scouts or Camp-Fire Girls, or receive religious instruction in the churches. This outside work is then ranked as an integral part of the school work.

It is this community coöperation which has particularly roused the interest of religious educators. It suggests to many of them a solution of the problems of religious education, and of separate denominational schools. Religion does not enter the Gary school in any form, not even in Bible reading and prayer. But children may go out, for one hour a day, two, three, or even four times a week, to classes in religious instruction, privately organized and supported by the various churches of the city. To meet the situation in Gary, the churches have in some instances engaged special instructors for these classes in religion. The Presbyterian, Methodist, and Christian churches are said to have united in engaging a teacher at a relatively high salary. Such coöperation not only insures the services of well-trained and liberal teachers, but must necessarily banish sectarian dogmatism from the teaching. In Gary, the Baptist, Roman Catholic, and Hebrew churches, besides the Y.M.C.A., are said to be giving this special instruction. In the Jefferson School more than half the children attend these classes at the churches. This feature of the Gary plan is one of the most interesting, and perhaps has the most far-reaching possibilities, in the way of transforming religious instruction in this country. This plan is characteristic of a school which seeks to meet the demands of the individual child, and to make everything in the community which is truly educational, or which, for any reason, parents and children believe to be genuinely educational, contribute to the life of the school community.

Since the other institutions have the same privileges as the churches, they are all given the opportunity in this plan of enlarging their effective resources. City schools which wish to adopt the Gary plan, but lack the ideal school plant or the varied facilities, may often avail themselves of the gymnasium, pools, playgrounds, etc., of near-by Y.M.C.A. or settlement houses, and use the public library and public playground, and thus acquire, by systematic coöperation with these other agencies, an effectively working Gary school. This plan has been adopted with great success in the case of the New York schools, a number of which are in the course of adopting the Gary plan, or many features of it. Their experience has shown that, by making the school a "clearing-house for children's activities," the social resources of all these communal institutions are vastly increased.

To sum up, the Gary school forms a children's community, which aims to provide the practical natural education of the old school, shop, and home which educated our forefathers. It is a necessary evolution and reorganization of the public school to meet the changed social and industrial conditions of the modern city. The school community, by providing a fourfold activity of work, study, and play, uses the children's time and keeps them from the demoralizing influence of the streets. In the "auditorium" it provides a public theater which may motivate all the work and study. By coöperating with all the community agencies which provide wholesome activities for children, it makes them all more valuable and effective. And by making the school as far as possible a self-sustaining community, it gives meaning and purpose to all the work, trains the children for the outside world, and cultivates the social virtues.

IV

PROGRAMS: THE SCHOOL AS A PUBLIC UTILITY

Schools such as those in Gary, with their elaborate equipment and special school enterprises, obviously require methods of financing radically different from those of the ordinary public school. It is, perhaps, this problem of how a small and relatively poor city like Gary could afford to maintain such schools that has aroused the interest of practical school men in the Gary plan. When the public schools were first started in the new town, the authorities found themselves in a peculiarly difficult situation, owing to the limited funds at hand and the demands of a rapidly increasing population. The conventional method of meeting the situation would have been to erect inferior buildings, to omit playgrounds, laboratories, workshops, to employ cheap teachers, to increase the size of classes, to limit the yearly term, or else to try to accommodate all the children in a few buildings on half-time work. These have been the methods which our large cities have almost universally felt themselves obliged to adopt when confronted with these problems of economy and congestion.

The other possible method — and this seems to be the unique contribution of the Gary plan to the economics of education — was to treat the public school as a public service, and apply to it all those principles of scientific direction which have been perfected for the public use of railroads, telephones, parks, and other "public utilities." The new city of Gary could create thoroughly modern, completely equipped school plants, and operate them so as to get the maximum of service from them. Superintendent Wirt and the school board believed that this plan would be the true economy.

Mr. Wirt says, "You can afford any kind of school desired if ordinary economic public-service principles are applied to public-school management. The first principle in turning waste into profit in school management is to use every facility all the time for all the people." Instead, therefore, of counting their financial resources and then deciding what limited educational facilities could be provided with them, the Gary authorities seem to have decided upon the ideal school plant desired to meet the needs of the modern city child, and then to have proceeded, by the ingenious application of principles well recognized in business and industry, to utilize their resources so as to support the desired facilities. The Gary plan has made evident the great wastes involved in the conventional methods of managing the public-school plant. All school men will agree with Superintendent Wirt when he says that "most certainly playgrounds, gymnasiums, and swimming-pools are good things for all children to have. I believe that gardens, workshops, drawing and music studios are good things for children to have. I believe that museums, art galleries, and libraries are good things for children to use systematically and regularly. In my judgment opportunities for religious instruction, for private instruction in music, and for assisting in desirable home work are good things for children. So also are coöperative classes between the academic school and the industrial activities of the school business departments, and between the school and industrial activities outside the school. In what way will the use of these facilities handicap a child in his efforts to secure an education?"

The answer is, of course, "in no way." These are the things the most advanced higher schools and wealthy private schools are providing for their pupils. School men may have desired to provide all these things for all the children of the elementary schools too, but rarely has economic skill combined with educational philosophy to bring such an ideal within the bounds of possibility. The Gary school seems to have found a way. It has actually realized the ideal, and made practicable that school-community life which other schools have only envisaged. It has found that any kind of school desired may be had if classrooms, auditoriums, playgrounds, etc., are in constant use all day long by all the children in alternating groups and out of school hours by adults.

"The modern city," says Superintendent Wirt, "is largely the result of the application of the principle of the common use of public facilities that we need for our personal use only part of the time. We are willing that other people use public services when we cannot use them. How many street-cars and what sort of service could we afford if each citizen had to have his own private street-car seat for his own exclusive use?" Yet the educational ideal in school management generally remains what is set forth in the report of the 1913 Part-Time Committee of the New York public schools, — "Every pupil is entitled to an individual seat and desk. The teacher is entitled to the exclusive possession of a classroom. . . ."

In the light of the Gary plan this ideal is absurd. It means, as has been discovered in the New York experience, that school facilities can never be made to catch up to school population. And it is absurd because it assumes that all persons in school want to do the same thing at the same time. But all "modern public conveniences are made possible only by their common use and the fact that we do not want to use the same public conveniences at the same moment. We are willing to have some one else use our public library, look at our pictures in our public museum, walk in our public park, sleep in our Pullman berth or in our hotel bedroom, or travel in our steamboat when we are otherwise engaged." It proves to be as financially prohibitive to attempt to provide an individual desk and seat for every school-child as it is to provide an individual seat for every citizen who may sit in the park. "The great masses of children in our city schools can never have ample play spaces, suitable auditoriums, gymnasiums and swimming-pools, workshops, libraries, museums, or even ordinary schoolrooms for study and recitation, if all children at the same time must be using each of these facilities separately." The more people use these public services, the cheaper they become for each one of us. And the more evenly the public use is distributed, the more valuable becomes the service to each one of us. "Increasing the number of persons using any public facility either under public or private ownership betters the service for all, provided the load can be uniformly distributed during operating hours. The problem with a public lighting or transportation service is to eliminate 'peak-loads' as far as possible."

We have had constantly before us the gradual extension of the principle of multiple service of public facilities. The Gary plan makes the public school the last of these public services to come under the operation of these principles. As generally managed the public school has not recognized these principles. The effect of its administrative methods, its rigid school hours, its uniform curriculum, its emphasis on academic work, has been rather to increase the "peak-loads" and thus inadvertently to increase the costs of operation. In many schools, the use of the "auditorium" does not average more than ten minutes a day for each day of the year, and the playgrounds barely an hour each day of the year. And for every hour that shops, etc., are empty, there is a waste and leakage, which would be permitted in no other public-service institution.

The Gary plan, therefore, has worked out a multiple use of the school plant in the most comprehensive form. By distributing classes in alternating groups, so that every department and room is in use as nearly as possible every hour of the eight-hour day, the "peak-loads" are prevented and the costs of operation reduced to the minimum. This system, variously called a "rotation-of-crops" or a "platoon" system, permits almost the actual doubling of the capacity of the school plant. Two duplicate schools may function together in the same building all day long. This "duplicate-school" plan is not, it must be observed, that used in some cities, where one school occupies the rooms for a few hours while the other remains at home, to take its turn in the rooms while the other goes out. That is merely a "part-time" scheme, and only accentuates the usual evils of fragmentary schooling and demoralizing street life. The Gary plan involves two distinct schools, known as the "X" and the "Y" schools, each of which has the entire program and the full day. The Gary plan, in other words, can accommodate twice the ordinary number in a school-building, not by shortening the time for each child, but actually by lengthening it.

How this plan works out in detail for a school unit of eight classes may be shown by the following program, which was used in the Jefferson School when Superintendent Wirt first came to Gary. The Jefferson School has been described as a conventional school-building, which was adapted to the Gary plan by the institution of shops, gymnasium, etc., and the conversion of classrooms into laboratories and studios. The program shows how a small eight-room school, ordinarily accommodating three hundred and twenty children (forty to a class), may, with a small auditorium, playground, attic gymnasium, and basement shops accommodate two duplicate schools of eight teachers each, with a total of six hundred and forty children. The first column gives the teachers, — grade teachers for the regular studies of the eight grades, and special teachers for the special activities. The second column gives the rooms where the work is conducted; the other columns give the distribution of time. "1X" means the first grade of the "X" school; "1Y" means the first grade of the "Y" school, etc. The program shows the ingenious distribution of classes throughout the school and throughout the course of the day,

— six hours in this case, to which one hour and a quarter must be added for lunch-time.

Studies		*Forenoon*		*Afternoon*	
Teachers	*Room*	*90 min.*	*90 min.*	*90 min.*	*90 min.*
1st Grade	Classroom	1X	1Y	1X	1Y
2d "	"	2X	2Y	2X	2Y
3d "	"	3X	3Y	3X	3Y
4th "	"	4X	4Y	4X	4Y
5th "	"	5X	5Y	5X	5Y
6th "	"	6X	6Y	6X	6Y
7th "	"	7X	7Y	7X	7Y
8th "	"	8X	8Y	8X	8Y
Music	Auditorium	1Y 2Y	1X 2X	3Y 4Y	3X 4X
Drawing	Basement	3Y 4Y	3X 4X	1Y 2Y	1X 2X
Literature . . .	Library	5Y 6Y	5X 6X	7Y 8Y	7X 8X
Science or manual arts	Basement	7Y 8Y	7X 8X	5Y 6Y	5X 6X
Physical education (2 teachers and principal) . . .	Attic	2Y 1Y	2X 1X	6Y 5Y	6X 5X
	Playground	4Y 3Y	4X 3X	8Y 7Y	8X 7X
	Attic	6Y 5Y	6X 5X	2Y 1Y	4X 3X
	Playground	8Y 7Y	8X 7X	4Y 3Y	2X 1X

According to this program, only eight regular schoolrooms are required for the sixteen classes. While these eight classrooms are occupied by the classes engaged in the regular studies, the eight other classes are engaged in special activities in other parts of the school plant, in basement shops, attic gymnasium, or playground. Half the day is given to the regular studies, and half to the special activities. The regular studies occupy two periods of ninety minutes each, one in the forenoon and one in the afternoon. The same amount of time is given to the special activities, but the ninety-minute periods are divided into two forty-five-minute periods. The time devoted to the regular studies is divided as the teachers see fit. Each teacher has but one class at a time, and the way in which the time is distributed between the arithmetic, reading, spelling, geography, history, etc., depends upon the needs of those in the class. It will be seen from the program that each class of the two duplicate schools has time not only for three hours a day of the traditional school studies, but for three hours of play and special activities besides. And since this is the daily program, each class gets this varied work, study, and play every day, and not, as is the case of the special work in most public schools, only once or twice a week. Thus, according to this program, the day's work for the third grade in the "X" school would be mapped out in this way, — regular studies, drawing or manual training, playground or gymnasium, lunch, regular studies, music, and playground again.

The sixth grade in the "Y" school has a program of physical education, music or literature, regular studies, lunch, play, science or manual arts, and regular studies again. The program shows not only how double the number of classes are accommodated, but how all are given a longer and more varied day than is possible in the ordinary school.

This program represents the simplest framework of the application of public-service principles to the daily school program, with its multiple use of facilities. It is known as the "Old Gary School Program," and has, of course, been much modified and refined and complicated as the need for flexibility and for the further departmentalizing of studies has arisen, and as it has had to be adapted to schools of different sizes. As here presented it does not include the high-school classes. The program of the complete school plant is much more elaborate. The "Old Gary School Program," however, contains the essential principles of the distribution of classes and of school time.

Since September, 1913, a new and more satisfactory program has been followed in the four larger Gary schools. The new school day is eight and one quarter hours in length, and the work is divided into four groups, as follows: —

Group	*Program*	*Hours*
1.	History and geography, English and mathematics	2
2.	Manual work, science, drawing, music	2
3.	Auditorium	1
4.	Play, physical training, application	2
	Lunch	$1\frac{1}{4}$

The first group of studies is conducted in the ordinary classrooms; the second group in the shops, laboratories, and studios; the third group in the auditorium; the fourth group in the gymnasiums, swimming-pools, playrooms and playgrounds. Four groups of children are simultaneously engaged in these four different departments throughout the day. If A represents one half of the classes of grades 1 to 4; B, one half of grades 5 to 8; C, the other half of grades 1 to 4; and D, the other half of grades 5 to 8 — then A and B together will represent the "X" school of our old program, and C and D together will represent the "Y" school, each school with its own corps of teachers and classes of all grades from 1 to 8. The new program for the duplicate school then works out in operation as follows. (The new day is an hour longer.)

Time	*Studies for*			
	Group 1 *	*Group 2*	*Group 3*	*Group 4*
8.15– 9.15......	A	B	—	C D
9.15–10.15......	B	A	C	D
10.15–11.15......	C	D	A	B
11.15–12.15......	D	C	Lunch-hour for A B	
12.15– 1.15......	A	B	Lunch-hour for C D	
1.15– 2.15......	B	A	D	C
2.15– 3.15......	C	D	B	A
3.15– 4.15......	D	C	—	A B

4.15– 5.00 Playgrounds, gymnasiums, and shops open for volunteers.

* See preceding table.

Since C D, or the "Y" school, has physical education the first hour in the morning, and A B, or the "X" school, has it the last hour of the afternoon, pupils in the "Y" school are permitted to come an hour later in the morning, and the pupils in the "X" school are permitted to leave an hour earlier in the afternoon. It will be observed from this program that only one fourth of the pupils are engaged in group 1 during any hour of the day. Four separate classes are, therefore, accommodated in each regular classroom. Consequently, the capacity of the school plant is four times that of the regular classrooms. But since a number of rooms which would otherwise be used for classrooms are used for laboratories and studios, the net capacity of the school plant operating under the new program is, as under the old program, twice the capacity of the total number of classrooms.

In the lower grades it is found desirable to use for formal physical training, half an hour out of the two hours assigned to group 2. An exchange is, therefore, made with the grammar and high-school grades, which are assigned to the regular classrooms for an additional hour of English and mathematics. In all grades the time assigned to group 4 is divided between the teachers of physical education and play, and the teachers of the subjects in groups 1 and 2. In the lower grades, teachers of the regular studies use their share of the time — one hour — in games and constructive plays that apply the subject-matter taught in the classes. This is the "application" work which is so distinctive a feature of the Gary school. It is planned systematically to give the formal work of the school opportunity for expression through activity. The music and literature teachers use the "application" period for folk-dances, musical games, dramatics, modeling in clay and sand, and for free imaginative play and construction. This "application" work is carried on informally in the broad halls or in corners of the playgrounds and playrooms. Whatever work has permanent value or interest may then be practiced for presentation in the "auditorium" period. The nature-study and science teachers use the application period for the care of the lawns, trees, shrubbery, the conservatories, the gardens, the animal pets. In the upper grades, mathematics teachers use this period for the practical measuring and planning of the various mechanical construction projects of the shops or grounds, or in practical accounting in connection with the clerical work of the school. In other words, it is in the "application" periods that that work is done which contributes to the school community life which has been described in the chapter on "The School as a Community."

In the lower grades, "application" takes largely the form of games. In the upper grades, the industrial and science work is used as the basis. Practical instruction is given by the shop and laboratory teachers, in addition to that given by the regular teachers. The special teacher has his pupils for one hour in the classroom, followed by two hours in the shop or laboratory where direct application is made of the theoretical instruction. This extra time is taken out of that assigned to group 4.

The division of time between the various activities in the new program therefore works out as follows: —

For grades 1 to 3: —

Language and mathematics	2 hours
Music, literature and expression, gymnastics	1 hour
Application	1 hour
Auditorium	1 hour
Lunch	1 hour
Manual work and nature-study	1 hour
Free play	1 hour

For the other grades, 4 to 8:—

Language, mathematics, history, geography	2 hours
Science and manual work	2 hours
Mathematics and English taught by shop and laboratory instructors	1 hour
Physical training and play	1 hour
Auditorium	1 hour
Lunch	1 hour

This is the new program for a school of eight grades. In the case of the complete school plant, such as those of the Emerson and Froebel Schools in Gary, with their twelve grades and their forty or more classes apiece, the program becomes much more complicated. But the division of time follows essentially the outlines given above, the high-school classes resembling the upper grammar grades' distribution of time and subjects.

The noteworthy thing about this program, apart from the ingenious and successful multiple use of the school plant it represents, is the equable distribution of time between the "regular studies" and the "special activities." In the Gary school, the "special work," more or less an appendage in the ordinary public school, is as regular as the "regular work." Yet the amount of academic work is no less than that in the ordinary schools. The various fundamental groups are participated in on equal terms. No subject is slighted, no age is slighted. The extended school day, which absorbs the "street and alley time" of the city child, affords ample opportunity for all activities. No activity is continued long enough to cause fatigue, while the constant daily cultivation of each activity provides the constant drill and the thoroughness of training which the ordinary school, with its short day and crowded curriculum, is compelled to slight. Such a program seems to be a highly rational distribution of school activities, as ingenious from the point of view of educational engineering as it is pedagogically sound. By treating the daily use of the schools as a public service, the Gary program obtains, for twice the number of children ordinarily accommodated, twice the number of facilities ordinarily provided. Each individual is immensely benefited because all are served. "The only reason why the public — that is, ourselves collectively — can afford to provide things for each of us individually that we cannot provide for ourselves privately, is that collectively we secure a multiple use of the facilities."

The same principles of administrative economy — an economy which creates rather than impoverishes — are applied to the yearly schedule as to the daily program. The Gary authorities find that they cannot afford to let their plant stand idle two or three months of the year, and are therefore working toward an all-year school. This effort coincides with a growing general belief that the long summer vacations not only demoralize the city child, but are a great waste of educational influence. At the present time state laws hinder the completion of the all-year plan. The Gary schools now have ten months of regular compulsory school, and ten weeks of voluntary vacation school, but they are working toward an organization of four quarters of twelve weeks each. This plan was approximated by Superintendent Wirt in the Bluffton schools before he came to Gary. Under this scheme pupils are required to attend any three of the four quarters, attendance in the remaining quarter being wholly voluntary. In Bluffton it was found that the attendance of the younger children for the summer quarter was greater than for any other quarter in the year. With the traditional term organization, many children are unavoidably absent in the winter on account of sickness and weather. Under the four-quarter arrangement, however, the allotted vacation of these children could be so organized as to include this absence and thus insure thirty-six weeks of schooling. "When people are given a chance," says Superintendent Wirt, "it is found that they do not want to go to school at the same time any more than they all want to travel at the same time."

The all-year school would not increase the cost of maintenance. For with the same number of pupils per teacher, the cost is the same whether the pupils are all taught together for thirty-six weeks, on the traditional plan, or whether only three quarters of them are taught at a time throughout a school year of forty-eight weeks.

The economies which this multiple use of school facilities effects are so large as to provide ample funds for all the special features of the Gary plan of education. These savings are in construction, in operation and maintenance, and in instruction. Savings in construction alone are very large. Since, under the duplicate-school plan, two complete schools may be accommodated in one building, the number of school plants may be greatly reduced. In the light of the Gary plan, therefore, those cities which are confronted with problems of school congestion are in the paradoxical situation of having, not too few buildings, but actually too many. Fewer and better plants would accommodate their children under the Gary plan. It must be remembered that the Gary schools at present have accommodations for many more children than there are children to use them, and this in spite of a phenomenal growth of population. The erection of a number of Gary unit plants is less expensive than the erection of a much larger number of ordinary school-buildings of the common school type. For the cost of building construction does not increase in proportion to the size of the building, and large sums may be saved on the fewer sites required. The diminution in the number of classrooms in the Gary school plant is a distinct source of economy, owing to the fact that the classroom is uniformly the most expensive portion of the school plant. The Gary experience seems to show that the best and completest unit school plant is also the cheapest. The plan of having the twelve grades under one roof avoids the reduplication of expensive equipment in several centers. And the self-sustaining industrial shops cut off an item of "vocational training" expense which most cities find almost financially prohibitive.

As for the costs of operation and maintenance, it is obvious that increasing the size of the school plant makes for economy. The cost of janitor service, administrative charges, heating, lighting, etc., are much reduced by consolidation. Nor, in order to effect these economies, need the size of the school plant be made so large as to make administration unwieldy. The largest Gary school plant, operating with all these economies, accommodates only twenty-seven hundred children, forty children to a teacher, while it is the intention to reduce the average number of children per teacher to thirty, and the building capacity to two thousand children.

Finally, the cost per pupil for instruction is decreased by the plan of specializing and departmentalizing the work, and thus eliminating overhead charges for supervisors. It should be pointed out again that *all these economies actually increase the educational efficiencies of the school.*

The figures show that the Gary school plan does not increase public expenditures for educational purposes. The Jefferson School, built before Superintendent Wirt came to Gary, and representing the common type of modern school-building, was erected at a cost of $90,000 to accommodate 360 pupils, with 40 pupils per teacher. This is a *per-capita* construction cost of $250, a cost exactly equal to that of a typical New Jersey High School recently erected at a cost of $125,000, with a maximum capacity of 500 pupils. The capacity of the Emerson School, constructed as an ideal Gary school plant, is 1800, with 30 pupils to a teacher. Its cost, with a large playground and the wealth of facilities already described, was about $300,-

000. The *per-capita* cost of construction was therefore $166. At its maximum capacity, with 40 pupils to the teacher, the *per-capita* cost of construction would be only $111, as against $250 for the Jefferson School, with no facilities. Further tables of comparative costs will be found in the Appendix.

The funds liberated by the application of these simple economical principles to public-school finance are so large as to give Gary the means to provide, as Superintendent Wirt says, "any kind of a school desired." Extraordinarily complete educational and recreational facilities may be furnished for all the people all the year round. Money is thus provided for an evening school for adults on an almost unprecedented scale. The Gary evening schools, held in the four largest school plants, four evenings a week throughout the regular school year from 7 to 9.30 P.M., have an attendance over two thirds that of the regular day schools. The cost of the evening school is only thirteen per cent of the day-school cost.

The evening schools of Gary resemble a people's university. Practically every study authorized by state law is given, and the bulletin of courses is like a university catalogue. All the shops, laboratories, studios, and classrooms are thrown open, either to repeat the day studies or to present more advanced work. All the work, industrial and academic, is open on equal terms to men and women. During 1914–15, 4300 students, representing all classes in the community, are said to have been enrolled in the Gary evening schools, with an average monthly enrollment of 3103. Over two thousand of the nine thousand voters at the last city election were said to be enrolled in the Gary evening schools. There are said to be more men over twenty-one attending evening schools in Gary than there are boys of all ages attending the day schools.

The Gary evening schools in the last year have achieved an even closer articulation of the work of the day and evening schools. A large number of short-unit courses were offered for busy men and women who wished particular branches of certain studies, and who could not remain in school to pursue their studies in the usual way. It has also been arranged to connect into group units the studies that bear upon a given industrial occupation, so that the school may correlate directly with all the occupations of the community, and the adult worker may come and secure the additional experimentation or theory which will help him in his work.

In addition to this instruction offered in academic and industrial work, to the evening pupils is given free use of the gymnasiums, pools, playgrounds, etc. The playgrounds are artificially lighted so that games may be played successfully at night. Playgrounds and swimming-pools are open on Sundays also, and the auditoriums for lectures, moving pictures, community forums, and the like. All wholesome social gatherings and entertainments are welcomed any evening of the week. The auditoriums are freely lent for political meetings, conferences, meetings of neighborhood or other private associations. The Gary school plant thus becomes in the fullest sense a social or community center. The "wider use of the school plant" here involves almost the widest possible use in the interests of all classes of the population; for the lavish Gary school plants contain equipments which serve the needs not only of children, but of all classes of adults as well, from the well-to-do woman who wishes to learn French to the sheet-metal worker in the mills.

By using the schools as a public service, the Gary educational authorities are thus able to provide for all the people facilities at no more expense than other communities are paying now for meager opportunities which do not even meet the needs of the children, while they leave the majority of adults entirely uninfluenced by the schools. "The private exclusive use of public-school facilities has meant and will continue to mean," says Superintendent Wirt, " that all of the people collectively can provide for only a part of their number."

The Gary school is evidently a genuine "public school" in a sense more "public" than is generally known. In many communities the public school is "still the old private school publicly supported." School boards often act as if they were trustees of private property. They gravely discuss "wider use of the school plant" as if this were some gracious extension of privilege instead of a public right. The public in many communities scarcely feel yet that the schools are their own. The Gary schools seem to have produced a different spirit. They are public in the same broad sense that streets and parks are public. They are used with the same freedom and lack of reserve. In such a community and such a school education would never be finished. Just as there is no break between common school and high school in the Gary plan, so there need be none between child and adult. The child would not "graduate," "complete his or her education," but would tend to drift back constantly to the school to get the help he or she needed in profession or occupation, or to keep on enjoying the facilities which even the wealthy private home would not be able or willing to afford. It is toward such a public educational ideal that the Gary plan seems to work. Toward this all the economies and ingenious schemes of organization are directed — toward making the public schools veritable "schools of the public."

V

ORGANIZATION

The distinctive features of organization in the Gary school are the separation of administrative from pedagogical supervision; the extension of departmental teaching throughout the entire school; the increased initiative and coöperation of the teaching force; the flexibility and simplicity obtained by the "helper" or "observer" system.

The school administration is vested in a single head, the superintendent of schools, who is appointed by the board of education of three members. In charge of each school-building is an executive principal, whose duties are concerned with program-making, with supervision of the pupil's schedules, with the general maintenance of order and discipline, and ordinary administrative work. He has no supervision of the instruction.

For all the schools there are two general supervisors of instruction, who oversee the teaching, work out the curricula in coöperation with the teachers, conduct examinations for promotion, make promotions or demotions after consultation with the teacher.

The industrial and manual-training shops are under the direction of a director of industrial work, who is also practical head of the school-building and repair department. The teacher-workmen in the shops are employed by him in the dual capacity of manual-training and industrial teachers and of regular workmen engaged in repair and construction. Each building has a head manual-training teacher, who supervises the work of the industrial classes, of the part-time classes, and acts as vocational adviser for the school's pupils. Gymnasium and swimming-pool attendants are employed by the head teachers of the physical education departments.

The departmental teachers in the head building (Emerson School) act as assistant supervisors of instruction in their subjects and have general oversight of the courses in their subjects as taught in the other buildings.

Departmental teaching is carried out in the Gary schools to an extent generally unrealized in other public schools. It is considered that, with the exception of the lowest grades, no arguments which apply to the institution of departmental teaching in the high school are inapplicable to the grades of the common school. The special activities undoubtedly call for specialists to conduct them. History, language, literature, mathematics can also be much better taught if the teacher can devote his or her attention to the particular methods and orientation of the respective subjects, and not be required to be equally at home in the technique of all of them. Teachers can rarely be found who are many-sided enough to teach well even all the common branches, without the special activities. The Gary schools, therefore, adopt for all, except the first two or three grades, what are practically advanced high-school or college methods of specialized teaching.

In these lowest grades all the regular subjects are taught by the one grade teacher; in the other grades practically all the subjects are departmentalized. A unit school plant which should have fifty-six classes, divided proportionately among the grades, in addition to the nurseries and kindergartens and

THE MACHINE SHOP AT THE EMERSON SCHOOL

special classes, would employ for grades 1 to 3, *sixteen* teachers, as follows: For English, mathematics, 8; for manual training, 2; for nature-study, 2; for music, 1; for expression, 1; for physical training, 2.

For grades 4 to 12, *forty-six* teachers would be employed: For English, 4; for mathematics, 2; for Latin, 1; for German, 1; for French, 1; for Spanish, 1; for history, 1; for fourth- and fifth-grade English, mathematics, history, and geography (either departmentalized or undepartmentalized), 8; for chemistry, 2; for botany, 2; for physics, 2; for zoölogy, 2; for freehand drawing, 2; for architectural drawing, 2; for mechanical drawing, 1; for music, 2; for expression, 2; for cooking, 1; for sewing, 1; for manual training (not including the industrial shops), 2; for physical training, 6. Four teachers would be employed in the kindergarten department. A unit plant of this size would require one executive building principal, and one supervisor of instruction. Two school nurses and a school physician would also be employed.

Such a distribution of the teaching force would be considered the ideal for a unit school plant of all grades, accommodating between fourteen hundred and twenty-two hundred and fifty children in two duplicate schools. It will be observed that this most careful specialization of teaching does not increase the number of teachers required. At least fifty-six teachers, with a number of special teachers, would be required in any school of fifty-six classes, run on an undepartmentalized plan. The Gary plan, therefore, without increasing the number of teachers, provides for a much higher expertness of service. Indeed, Superintendent Wirt has worked out a form by which a school of thirty-two classes would only require thirty-two teachers, including the special teachers, and with most of the work departmentalized.

Programs may be arranged for schools with any number of classes. The number of classrooms and teachers required will be approximately as follows, including supervisors, special teachers, librarians and playground instructors: —

A 12-class school requires 8 classrooms and 12 teachers.
A 24-class school requires 15 classrooms and 23 teachers.
A 36-class school requires 22 classrooms and 33 teachers.
A 48-class school requires 29 classrooms and 43 teachers.
A 60-class school requires 36 classrooms and 54 teachers.
A 72-class school requires 43 classrooms and 64 teachers.

In the 72-class school, 43 classrooms and 54 teachers are required, in addition to the provision for auditorium, playrooms, and library. For this work 10 teachers are required, making a total of only 64 teachers for 72 classes. The traditional elementary school requires 72 teachers and 72 classrooms for 72 classes; the manual-training shops and the manual-training teachers are extra. In addition there would be librarians in branch public libraries, playground directors in public playgrounds, and special teachers as supervisors of music, drawing, physical training, manual training, and nature-study. Often in the traditional school 80 or more persons are employed for the instruction of 72 classes, not including the building principal and assistants.

An important feature of the teacher organization in the Gary school is the division into senior and junior teachers, or head teacher and assistant teacher. Since each classroom accommodates two teachers according to the duplicate-school plan, the teacher who has been longer in service is designated as head teacher. The less experienced teacher acts under her direction. The head teachers, for instance, in the "X" school may visit and criticize the work of the assistant teachers in the "Y" school during the last hour of the day when the "X" school is not in session. Similarly the junior teacher in the "Y" school may visit the work of the "X" school during the first hour. Inexperienced or weak teachers may thus be developed under the direction of the more experienced. New teachers are thus being constantly trained in the new régime and spirit of the Gary school. The school is thus made an extension of the normal or training-school for teachers. The teachers continue to learn as well as the pupils. The question how teachers are to be procured for the new demands which the Gary plan puts upon them is thus answered. The school itself trains the teachers.

The responsibilities of the teachers for the auditorium period have been discussed. Under the old Gary plan each auditorium period was in charge of one teacher who acted as assistant principal. The teachers alternated in organizing the dramatic and other features of the auditorium work. Recently Superintendent Wirt has decided that this auditorium work functions better if it is specialized. In the new 72-school program, four teachers give their time exclusively to the auditorium exercises. One teacher has charge of the music; one has charge of the art, literature, history, civics, and current events; one has charge of the presentation of material relating to the science work; and one has charge of the presentation of the material relating to the shops and industries. In a properly equipped auditorium, with stereopticon lantern, motion-picture machine, stage, player-piano, organ, and phonograph, the auditorium teachers can do many things better with large numbers of children than the regular teachers can do with small numbers. The regular classroom teachers are expected to coöperate in this frequent presentation of work by their classes in the auditorium in order to use it as a place for "application" work and for motivating the academic work of the school.

In the new program, the "application" work is also specialized. Experience has shown that some teachers have a special talent for this imaginative and constructive side of teaching, and prefer to devote their entire time to it. In this scheme, the "application" teachers have six classes daily out of a total of twelve classes in each of their respective groups. They are thus able to meet each of the twelve classes of their respective groups every other day, week, month, or term. Or these teachers may select from each of the groups of three classes the pupils who need special work in language and mathematics, and meet these pupils every day. For the average pupil all of the opportunity necessary to make an application of his language and mathematics is provided in the regular manual-training, drawing, music, and expression classes. The "application" teachers meet their respective classes in the manual-training, drawing, music, and expression rooms. The facilities of these special rooms are used for "application" purposes. The "application" teachers are expected to make suggestions to the special teachers of these subjects concerning the opportunities to teach language and mathematics through the "application" opportunities of the regular work of their respective subjects. Each "application" teacher may be constituted the head of a group of eight teachers. The "application" teacher is the correlating agent for all the work of the twelve classes; also she works with all of the twelve classes as a constructive examiner, and is constantly placing before the children real problems of the type that the world of industry, business, and citizenship will place before them when they leave school. She may not be able to present these problems as well as the world will present them later, but the immediate and daily reaction while the child is in school should be invaluable in preparing him for meeting the more difficult problems which arise when he has completed his school course.

Class periods may be 40 or 50 or 55 minutes instead of 60. Teachers have six hours in school with 60-minute periods, five and one-half with 55-minute periods, and five hours with 50-minute periods. Pupils have a school day of seven, six and one-half, and six hours respectively, in addition to an hour for luncheon. The playground teachers are on duty an additional hour. Each teacher has an hour a day free for her own work. When her day is finished, she is supposed to leave the building. It is expected that all paper work, as well as all the work of the children, will be done in school. The purpose is to make the teacher's day only six hours, without the burden of extra time at home.

An interesting extension of this teacher-organization plan is the new training course for outside teachers or principals who are desirous of studying the Gary school plan and teaching methods. Visiting teachers and principals are allowed, at a fee, to attach themselves as assistants to teachers or principals, and follow the work through a course of weeks or months, in exactly the same way that the small child acts as "helper" or "observer" to the older child in the laboratory or shop or the junior to the senior teacher. The fee goes to the teacher or principal who instructs the visitor. This novel way of teaching the principles of the Gary school, not by lectures, but by direct practical assistance on the part of the visitor, is typical of that insistence upon "learning by doing" which is the keynote of the Gary instruction.

The Gary plan acts on the theory that the good teachers should be given initiative and responsibility, while the inexperienced and weak teachers should be trained into initiative and responsibility. The usual plan in school systems is to make the experienced and inexperienced, strong and weak, coördinate with one another, and all subordinate to the supervisor or superintendent. The Gary plan thus secures the utmost from the good teachers, and trains the poor ones.

Instead of employing special "visiting teachers," as is done in many school systems, the teacher in the Gary school is given the responsibilities of the "visiting teacher" by being made a "register teacher" for a subdivision of the school district. In this way cases of maladjustment to school, home, or neighborhood conditions may be met. The school population of the city is geographically districted in such a way that each district holds about fifty families. The children in a district are assigned, irrespective of age or grade, to one of the grade teachers. Each "register teacher" meets her group once a week for general conference. She gives out the monthly reports. Failure in self-control, irregular attendance, tardiness, and other matters are reported to her. No child is excused from class without her permission, and she is expected to call at the homes of the children when necessary or to meet their parents at the school. Each "register teacher" holds the same children from class to class as long as they live in the district. She corresponds almost exactly to what is known as the "faculty adviser" of the college student, a guide and friend for the general conduct of school life and for difficulties that arise. The "register teacher" is a sort of disciplinary and sociological overseer for a group of children living in the same neighborhood. She has a set of blanks which in fact provide a basis for a complete sociological survey of her district. These she is supposed to fill in, as facts about living conditions, etc., come to her attention. It seems evident that this work, while exacting, involves no more than a teacher should know. No more valuable sociological training could be imagined for the intelligent and progressive teacher. Such work relates her at once to the general community life, and makes her profession of a far more serious importance than is usually given to the grade teachers in the public schools. This work is typical of the demands for a new initiative and intelligence that the Gary plan makes upon the teachers, and also of the immense educative value of these demands.

The effort is constantly made in the Gary schools to bridge the gap between teacher and pupil. An important recent innovation is the institution of "teachers' assistants." Students in the sixth, seventh, and eighth grades have ten weeks for drawing, ten weeks for science, ten weeks for shopwork, and ten weeks for service as "teachers' assistants." The students act as laboratory and studio assistants only in the departments in which they have a special interest. Three or four students assist the science teachers, three or four the drawing teachers, and three or four the shop teachers. Playground teachers, auditorium teachers, music teachers, etc., have as assistants the students especially interested. Each student can, therefore, receive twenty weeks of work in the department in which he has a special interest. Many teachers confess that the first year of teaching gave them a much clearer grasp of the subjects they taught than they were able to secure as students. From the point of view of scholarship, the teachers' assistants learn more by acting in this rôle for a limited time than they could learn by using the time for additional study. They not only learn how to take initiative and assume responsibility, but they enable the teacher to do much more effective work with the regular classes.

This same fundamental principle of organization is applied to the pupils themselves in their relations with one another. Fourth- and fifth-grade pupils are considered too old for the primary manual training and nature-study, and not quite old enough to use profitably the laboratories and workshops as independent students. They are, therefore, assigned as assistants to students in the higher classes. These children in this way learn more by working with the older students than they can be taught in separate classes by themselves. Not only does the younger child learn by helping the older and watching him and asking questions of him, but the older learns by being required to answer the questions and make the younger child understand what he is doing in shop or laboratory. The object is to make the Gary school, in the words of Superintendent Wirt, "as much as possible like a large family wherein the younger children are learning consciously and unconsciously from the older, and the latter from contact with the younger children are learning to assume responsibility and take the initiative. Some one has said that we send our boy to school, but his playmates, not the school faculty, educate him. This is true because in the conventional school the faculty does not utilize the playmates as assistant instructors." This "helper" system has proved to be one of the most valuable features of the Gary schools.

For the pupil, organization means a degree of flexibility and individual instruction extraordinary for a public school. Except in the lowest grades, the pupils are classified by subjects as well as by grades, so that practically college methods obtain. Each pupil has his own schedule or program, just as the college student has. The executive principal corresponds to the college registrar in supervising these individual records. The pupil is promoted by subjects and not by grades, and may be promoted or demoted at any time by the supervisor of instruction, acting with the teacher. Grades, therefore, represent merely years of schooling and not classes which are promoted as units. Each regular class has a maximum register of forty, but the class does not work as a unit, any more than a college class of sophomores works as a unit. Some are taking one group of subjects, some another. The work is thus done largely in small groups, or even as individuals. The great wealth of equipment and the economical use of time permit a large amount of practically individual instruction.

The students of each grade are classified into three groups — rapid, normal, and slow workers. The rapid workers can easily complete the twelve years' course in ten years. They may then enter college at sixteen years of age. The great majority of the Gary pupils who go to college actually come from this rapid-working group. The normal workers complete the course in twelve years, and the slow workers in fourteen. Many of the slow workers do not attempt to complete the course, but specialize in the industrial departments. This grouping contemplates the recognition of differences in the mental endowments and ambitions of children of the same age, so that means are provided for the shortening of school life for some children and the lengthening of it for others. Every child is, as far as possible, working along with his equals, so that the bright child is not held back and rendered listless by the presence of slower members in the class, nor is the slow child discouraged by the competition of the brighter ones. Every pupil may go as fast as he can, and may specialize on the work which he can best do. The presence of a great variety of activities makes it possible for the children who falter on their intellectual work to give more attention to the manual or artistic or physical work in which they may excel.

A special investigation was made in 1914 into the regrading of the pupils of two ninth-grade algebra classes in the Emerson School. The results of regrading the classes into rapid and slow workers showed marked improvement in the interest displayed in the algebra work, especially on the part of the slow workers. No failures were reported among the rapid workers, and only three among the slow workers, and these were due to absence from class. The total class average for the slow division was in three months raised five per cent. In the Jefferson School, which has been operated on the Gary plan longer than any other school, fifty-two per cent of the children are one or more years *ahead* of their normal grades.

Many features of the Gary plan afford extraordinary opportunities for extra assistance in study and work. The pupil may take extra work in a subject during a proportion of his play, auditorium, or shop hours. If he is a member of the "X" school, he may get the same lesson repeated for him the same day by attending the parallel class in the "Y" school held at a different hour. He may come to the voluntary Saturday school and get extra coaching from the teacher, and the vacation school provides additional opportunity to make up back work. No home work is allowed, except to a small extent in the high-school grades. The long school day, and the freedom which the teacher has to distribute her time and to conduct supervised study, obviate the necessity for carrying books away from the school. Since the state law does not authorize the schools to provide free textbooks, these must be provided by the pupil, or, as in the case of most of the Gary classes, bought by the school and loaned co-operatively to a number of classes. Since home work is not permitted, the books may be kept in the school and distributed to the classes as they require them.

The headquarters of the pupil in the school are not in the classroom, as in other public schools. It is the teacher and not the class which is assigned to the room. The teacher remains in the room and the pupils go to him or her, moving about individually from class-room, shop, laboratory, etc., according to the printed schedule card which each pupil holds. The child's headquarters is the spacious lockers which line the corridors in the basements.

Each child has a private locker for books, papers, and wraps. Strictly speaking, the pupil in the Gary school, except in the lowest grades, has no "teacher," except the "register teacher." The departmental system gives him many teachers, but no teacher. This system and the self-governing responsibility for his own schedule is intended to cultivate initiative and responsibility on the part of the pupil. It brings him from an early age into contact with different personalities, gives him the benefit of expert teaching and a variety of movement and exercise. The introduction of these free college methods into the common school is, in the light of public-school practice, a daring experiment, but the Gary school experience seems to show that it is quite possible to give the younger children a large measure of freedom and individuality of treatment.

Most of the schedules of the pupils are arranged with reference to the requirements of the state course of instruction, specialization not being permitted, of course, except in the higher grades, or where some special weakness causes repeated failure. Yet the Gary schools have about twenty per cent of special students who do not intend to finish the course and are specializing in some departments. But since, owing to the individualization of schedules, every pupil is in a sense a "special student," the presence of this large number of students causes no administrative confusion, nor are the special students — as would be the case in many schools operated on a uniform plan — marked off invidiously from those who are following the more regular course.

The segregation of sexes which the visitor finds in some of the Gary schools and courses is not the result of any prejudice against coeducation. (All the activities are open equally to boys and girls alike, so that girls are found in the printing-shop and in the wood-working classes, etc.) It is due to the effort to give each boy and girl what he or she needs. The organization of many classes, such as play, gymnasium, personal hygiene, and the manual activities which do not appeal to the girls, or the domestic science which does not appeal to the boys, required this unisexual classification, and sometimes it has been retained to avoid the break-up of classes in related subjects.

An example of this effort to provide for all kinds of students in the Gary school is the first-year college work which is offered to students who wish to remain in the school for post-graduate work. The Gary school endeavors thus to overlap the college, just as it has made the common school dovetail into the high school, and the day school into the evening school. When the Gary high-school students have come up through the Gary schools, it is hoped to be able to send students from the local schools at the age of eighteen so prepared that they may complete the ordinary college course in two years.

A word should be said about the interrelation of this flexibility of schedule with the "helper" system. The choice of what subjects the pupil shall study is not as willful and anarchical as it may seem. In the lower grades the regular studies are, of course, prescribed. English, arithmetic, history, and geography must be studied by all, with the attendant "application" and "auditorium" work. All must have physical education, music and expression, and some form of manual and scientific work. The courses in science, industrial work, and music and expression, below the high school, are taken in alternation. Each occupies one third of the school year. The individual choice of the pupil comes in what science or what shop work he or she will take. The beginning is not by chance, but really the result of a natural process of selection by the child. All the early years are made a sort of unconscious prevocational school in which the child tries out his interests and powers. Things are neither forced on him nor aimlessly selected. The child in kindergarten or first three grades moves about the halls and corridors. Since the shops and studios and laboratories are not segregated, but distributed over the building, so that all seem equally significant, the child has every opportunity to become familiar with them. His curiosity is aroused, and, unaided, he is tempted to peer in through the glass doors and windows, and wonder what the older children are doing. When the child has reached the fourth grade, he already has an idea of what activity interests him, and what he would like to try. Fourth- and fifth-grade children then go in as helpers to the seventh-, eighth-, and ninth-grade students in shops, studios, and laboratories. If the child finds the work does not interest him, he still has a chance to try some other work, and thus gradually sifts out what is likely to be valuable to him for a vocation or avocation. If he has special skill, he may specialize in the higher grades. Such a plan seems to be admirably devised to bring out whatever capacities there are in the pupils, and to insure almost automatically their interest in work which in many schools is mere unintelligent drudgery.

Vocational guidance in such a system is simple and effective. The "auditorium" teacher, in charge of the presentation of material relating to the shops and industries, is able to give information as to the desirability of the several trades and industries as occupations. For example, the school plumber may prepare with his students a plumbing outfit for an ordinary dwelling or apartment, and give a lesson on the way in which plumbing should be cared for in the home. The plumbing instructor may know much about plumbing, but very little about presenting his information to a large body of students. The "auditorium" teacher would assume the responsibility of supervising such auditorium presentations in order that they might be dramatically effective. The day that the plumber and his students present the advantages and disadvantages of plumbing as a trade, the teacher of industries may announce to the boys in "auditorium" period that for the remainder of the week any boy may be excused for a personal consultation with him concerning the desirability of joining a class in plumbing. Students are thus directed in their shop assignments by this "auditorium" teacher of industries. Vocational guidance is thus made possible as far as it is probably wise to undertake such guidance in the school at present. Such a plan directs the mechanically inclined among the children by enlisting their interest and then their will. The "auditorium" teachers for the other activities may also act as advisers in the same way. Teacher and pupil thus coöperate, not in any haphazard fashion, but systematically, in studying the various activities with a view to their future use as a vocation. Such an attitude not only organizes and motivates the work, but gives it seriousness and purpose. Every detail of organization in the Gary school is devised to make the pupil as well as the teacher an integral part of the school life, not only in its own meaning, but in its relation to the outside world.

VI

CURRICULUM: LEARNING BY DOING

The Gary curriculum, in spite of its many special features, is neither eccentric nor overcrowded. It follows the regular course of study laid down for Indiana schools by the State Department of Public Instruction. Students who follow the full course may be ready to enter college at the age of sixteen. The additional facilities of the Gary schools are not gained at the expense, therefore, of the ordinary course of education. They are made possible through a more ingenious distribution of time throughout a longer school day, and by an integration and interrelation of subjects which tend to vitalize them all.

The regular studies in the lower grades are conducted along the conventional lines, with the addition of the "application" work which has been described. The English work is further vitalized through the employment of special teachers for "expression," who alternate with the special teachers of music.

"Expression" is a mixture of elocution and dramatics. The aim of the instruction is evidently to bring the pupils to read and speak with more intelligence and appreciation than is usually done. It is to give the training which will bear fruit in increased expressiveness in all the studies of the school, in all writing and reciting, in "auditorium" and "application" work. So far, owing to the peculiar requirements of talent in the teachers and on account of the lack of good American elocutionary and dramatic tradition, the enterprise can scarcely be called more than a frank and important experiment. For the Gary curriculum with its emphasis on self-activity, such training in expressiveness is essential, and it can be depended upon to improve rapidly in quality as the children and teachers catch the spirit of the schools and get the practice of "auditorium" and "application" work.

The importance of the equable division of time between regular studies and special activities has already been discussed. An important feature of the Gary teaching is the avoidance of that excessive subdivision of subjects which has affected curriculum-making in many schools. History and geography are here uniformly taught together; language, grammar, spelling, reading, and writing are taught as much as possible together as English; physiology is taught in connection with zoölogy. Since the teacher is left much initiative in the distribution of her time, she may emphasize and correlate the different studies as she finds necessary. All the English branches are taught constantly in connection with the other studies. The history or physics class may begin with a spelling-lesson. Compositions in science or history, or the brochures issued by the science departments, are supervised by the English teacher. We have seen how the shop and commercial instructors give special work in practical English and mathematics. The effort is constant in the Gary curriculum to teach a subject, not as an isolated body of subject-matter, but as knowledge which may bear on any or all the other departments of the school community.

Studies are taught also with as much bearing as possible on the social activities of the larger city community. The subject-matter in the history and geography classes is really "The Sociological World we Live in," and textbooks, histories, atlases, globes, newspapers, and magazines become the reference sources and the materials for understanding that world. The working-out of such principles must, of course, be a matter of experimentation by able teachers, and the work cannot be described in any formal manner. Illustrations of some of the successful methods can, however, be given. The history room in the Emerson School, for instance, is found by the visitor to be almost smothered in maps and charts, most of them made by the children themselves, in their effort to "learn by doing," and to contribute their part to the school community. A large Indiana ballot, a chart of the State Senate, a diagram of the state administration, a table showing the evolution of American political parties, with many war maps and pictures, covered the walls. The place is a workshop rather than a classroom, with broad tables for map-drawing, and a fine spread of papers and magazines. The ninth-grade Gary children

THE HISTORY ROOM AT THE EMERSON SCHOOL

are, in fact, conducting what some progressive colleges have introduced as "laboratory work in history."

When the writer visited the school, the town of Gary was waging a campaign for a new water-front park. The history class had for some weeks been using this public issue as a text for their work. They had been studying "The City: A Healthful Place in Which to Live (with special reference to parks)." Outlines had been worked up from reference books in the school branch of the public library. These were read to the class and discussed by them. Such a course became almost one in town-planning, one of the most fascinating and significant of current social interests, and one which packs into itself a maximum of historical, sociological, and geographical information. Such a course provided an admirable motive for a review of history from a practical local point of view which all the intelligent pupils could appreciate. The outline follows: —

The City: A Healthful Place in Which to Live: Emphasis on Parks

1. Athenian recreation centers.
2. Roman opportunities for recreation.
3. Mediæval cities: England.
4. Mediæval cities: Continental Europe.
5. The modern British city.
6. Modern cities in Argentina, Chile, Brazil.
7. The large German city.
8. The small German city.
9. Paris, and the smaller French cities.
10. Colonial cities of America.
11. American cities during the last quarter of the eighteenth century.
12. American cities before the Civil War.
13. American cities from the Civil War to the twentieth century.
14. American cities in the twentieth century.
15. How smaller cities are replanning.
16. Parks in large American cities.
17. The city-planning conference.
18. Statistics showing total area of city, and percentage of park space.
19. Playgrounds of Chicago and New York.
20. The Gary plan of schools and playgrounds on the same site.

The class in ancient history, owing to a belief on the part of the instructor that no child should be allowed to leave school without a background of modern affairs, devotes one day a week to contemporary history. A weekly digest of the ten most important events is kept in the history notebook, arranged, three for foreign events, three for national events, and four for local. Reports are prepared and read upon assigned magazine articles, especially from the *Literary Digest*, *Outlook*, and *Independent*. Everything is thus done to get the clue of historical study from the interesting events around the pupils. History is studied as much as possible backward, instead of forward.

In 1912–13 the classes in modern history became interested in the past of the Balkan nations, in order to understand the reason for their alliance against the Turkish Empire. A digression was, therefore, made to clear this point, and to vitalize thereby the history of the related European countries. The next year a similar interest was kindled in Mexico and our relations with the Spanish-American republics. During the past year the history instructor has found the study of the last two centuries of western Europe to move along without effort, owing to the interest in the great war.

Such a study of history clearly obviates the

necessity of any separate study of "civics." History and geography taught in this way become part of one's general information. Magazines and newspapers are freely used. The systematic reading of the best weeklies and papers surely is an important training, in an age of so much cheap and worthless reading-matter.

One history class had been making a comparison of Athenian with Gary education. This is another illustration of that constant effort to make the pupils realize the meaning of what they are doing and what is around them. The effort of the Gary education is to make the child acquainted with the purposes of his school. He is not taught as an inferior who must take without question wisdom from immensely superior teachers, but as an equal and democratic citizen of his school community, learning wherever and whenever he can. The ancient history class had for its motto: "To improve its members as American citizens by a study of the experiences of the ancient peoples." It would be difficult to imagine a more admirable reason for historical study than this phrase, the natural expression of the Gary child who wrote the constitution for the class organization. Such "social introspection" is as rare an intellectual quality as it is valuable.

The history classes in the lower grades use sand-tables to reproduce the topography of the localities which are being studied, or to describe the progress of some battle or invasion. One of the pupils in 1912 constructed with his own hands in the wood-working shops a miniature Roman temple about five feet in length, the plans of which he had worked out from the descriptions in the histories. These classes often engage in debates, and the written reports which are sufficiently interesting are read in "auditorium," and often printed in the local newspapers. Bulletin boards are placed in the hall for displaying important clippings. The pupils bring these, and classify them under the headings, — foreign news, American news, state, city, and county news, pictures and cartoons, and items on the special topics that are being studied. The history classes have charge of a small historical museum in the corridors, which contains a loan collection of Indian relics and of pottery from Central America.

The teaching of science occupies a unique place in the Gary schools. Just as the history and geography are taught as clues to the social and political world around the pupil, so the science is used to acclimatize him to the natural world. The theory is that children should commence the study of the sciences while their minds are still plastic and their interest in natural phenomena keen. The persistent questions which the child asks are attempts to get an understanding of the world he lives in. Unless these questions are answered, his interest is apt to wane as he grows older. And unless he acquires a familiarity with nature that is accompanied by true scientific information, he is apt to get only a satisfied feeling of knowledge without any true appreciation.

Science in the Gary schools, consequently, goes beyond the simple nature-study taught now in most elementary schools. The child has experience with the laboratory at an early age. The smaller children from the third, fourth, fifth, or sixth grades go into the chemistry, physics, botany, and zoölogy laboratories as "helpers" or "observers" to the work of the high-school classes. On the theory that "children are natural scientists" they are allowed contact with apparatus and materials. It is said, in fact, that experience shows the smaller children to be as careful as the older, and actually to cause less breakage and damage.

The science classes in the lower grades are taught neither in formal recitation nor in formal laboratory work, but in a combination which the instructors describe as "experience meetings." Pupils and teacher meet on common ground to exchange ideas about their experiences in dealing with natural phenomena. The outside world is treated as a great laboratory, and these "experience meetings" are used to interpret the children's experiences in terms of scientific principles. There are demonstrations by the children, assisted by the teacher; a little individual laboratory work; and considerable vocal reading from textbooks and scientific story-books.

The Gary science instructors believe that much time and money have been wasted in the teaching of science in high schools, owing to the elaborate methods which have treated the students as if the purpose was to make professional scientists of them all. Children, it is believed in Gary, cannot resort to the detailed research methods of scientists, but must have quick answers and quick results. There is a waste of energy in trying to duplicate in the laboratory the fundamental experiences of life which the children are constantly seeing outside in the great laboratory of nature.

The care of the flowers and plants and gardens, the care of the animals in the zoo, and the study of their habits offer endless concrete material for building up the theoretical side of botany and zoölogy. The pupils are trained to observe and to write down what they see. One class in zoölogy last year made an illustrated booklet descriptive of the school zoo. The text was written by the pupils, the photographs prepared by them, and then the booklet was tastefully printed in the school printing-shop by the pupils themselves. The result was a charming brochure, in which not only the pupils themselves, but the whole school could take pride and pleasure. Such scientific study becomes an intimate and vital part of the entire school life.

For the physics classes, the lighting, heating, and ventilating systems of the school afford a practical textbook. In the Jefferson School, where the industrial shop is built around the boiler room, the heating plant becomes an integral part of the shop. The physics classes study the climate and the weather. They study particularly the principles of the machines used in the different shops. Each shop may thus act as an extension of the physics laboratory. Classes of even the smaller children are sent to take apart machines like the bicycle, cream-separator, lawn-mower, and explain the construction. The automobile and motor-cycle provide many practical lessons. An old automobile which needs tinkering up is considered in the Gary school to be almost a physics laboratory in itself. The writer witnessed a physics class of twelve-year-old girls who, with their nine-year-old "helpers," were studying the motor-cycle. With that disregard for boundaries which characterizes all Gary education, the hour began with a spelling-lesson. The names of the parts and processes of the machine were rehearsed orally and then written. After the words were learned, the parts of the machine were explained by the instructor while the class spelled the words over again. Their memory of certain physical principles, such as vaporization, evaporation, were called again into play. Then the instructor set the motor-cycle going, the girls again describing its action. When this had been thoroughly gone over, the class copied from the blackboard sentences describing the processes and parts, but omitting certain crucial words which the pupil had to supply. The intense vivacity and interest of the little group, the intelligence with which these small children grasped the principles involved, made the lesson seem a model of expert teaching. It was an excellent illustration of the way concrete processes may be used to build up scientific knowledge. It is interesting to notice that no distinction is made between boys and girls in their science work.

This lively interest in scientific processes may have unexpected results. The story is told of a high-school boy who, while the board of education was discussing means of fire-prevention, made an investigation of methods and processes which was so excellent that it was forthwith adopted by the board.

This incident is typical of the way in which the scientific work in the schools may correlate with the wider social community. Just as the history classes may bring the pupil into touch with the political life outside the school, so the physics and chemistry class may connect him with the industry of the community and with those public services into which scientific processes enter. A boy, for example, brings to the chemistry class a bag of low-grade iron ore which he has found in the vicinity. The class, under the direction of the teacher, constructs a simple electric furnace and reduces the ore. This experiment is then used as the basis for a study of the great steel industry upon which the city of Gary is founded.

A part of the chemistry work makes a direct contribution to the city. Gary has the good fortune, or the good sense, to have as chemistry teacher in the Emerson School the man who acts as municipal chemist for the city. As a result, the school laboratory becomes an extension of the municipal laboratory. The high-school chemistry pupils assist the chemist just as the smaller children assist them. With the chemist-instructor the pupils test the city water and the various milk supplies. Under the sanitary inspector they visit, as part of their "application" work, dairies, factories, bakeries, food-stores. Last year the class issued a "Milk Bulletin," containing general information, with reports of their tests. The various articles were recorded as part of the English composition work, and the bulletin was printed by the pupils in the school printing-shop. In quality these bulletins seemed scarcely inferior to what an agricultural school might issue. On their inspection rounds, the class takes samples of sugars and candies from the various shops of the town, and tests them in the laboratory for purity and for the use of harmless coloring matter. Another class experiments with the soft drinks sold in the town, testing their composition, and studying physiological effects. The children are practically deputy food-inspectors, and make their reports on the official blanks. It is said that the result of this sort of inspection is that in a prosecution for violation of the pure-food laws in Gary a case has never been lost.

The children test also the materials supplied to the schools, the coal, cement, etc., to see if they come up to the specifications. They are not only using the things around them for practical textbooks, but they are able to turn their knowledge immediately into work which is immensely beneficial, not only to themselves, but to the whole community. The value of enlisting pupils in this inspection work, of training them to observe and criticize and test the physical conditions under which they live, is incalculable. For even a small proportion of children to get this scientific-deputy-inspector habit, and to get used to thinking in terms of qualitative and quantitative tests, would evidently have some effect upon political and social conditions. Such scientific training makes science an integral part of life, not only a knowledge of how natural forces and materials behave, but also a command of technical resources in making them behave in desirable ways. The pupils in such a school, from their earliest years, get a correct appreciation of the value of science in ameliorating conditions and in improving the healthfulness and security of the community in which they live.

The Gary curriculum seems to represent a determined effort to break down the distinction between the "utilitarian" and the "cultural." All the subjects are taught, as far as possible, in concrete ways which shall draw upon familiar experience and teach the child by making him do something. That something is made, as far as possible, an activity which will enhance the life of the school community, or contribute to the social community. These activities are "utilitarian," but they are at the same time profoundly educative. Principles are never lost sight of in practice. The artistic and academic work take equal rank with the manual. Both "cultural" and "utilitarian" are, in fact, subjected to the "*social.*" This is the key note of the Gary education.

VII

DISCIPLINE: THE NATURAL SCHOOL

THE problems of discipline in a Gary school are essentially different from those of public schools run on the usual semi-military plan. The large degree of coöperation between teachers and pupils and between pupils, the emphasis on laboratory, shop, and "application" work, where freedom of movement and conversation is essential, produces a more natural atmosphere, and a certain amount of genuine if unconscious self-government. The children in the Gary schools are generally conscious of the unique features of their school; they understand what the school is trying to do. This sense, and their pride in its fame, cultivate an admirable school spirit denied to those schools which are operated on conventional lines.

The organization of the Gary school permits the reduction of formal discipline to a minimum. It allows the teachers to dispense with disciplinary rules against whispering, with formal punishments, with formal marks or demerits for conduct. The frequent change of activity, with opportunities for exercise throughout the day, prevents the children from becoming nervously overwrought. They thus escape irritability and aimless boisterousness when left to themselves. The "application" and shop work compel attention, so that the child is kept busy and interested, and the mischievousness that arises from idleness or distracted attention is avoided. As Professor Dewey says, "Trained in doing things, the child will be able to keep at work and to think of the other people around him when he is not under restraining supervision." When the teacher's rôle changes from preceptor to that of helper, it is obvious that what is needed in the classroom is not so much perfect quiet and military order as freedom of expression and spontaneity.

Visitors to the Gary schools bear witness to the peculiarly beneficial effects of this absence of formal discipline. The free and individual way in which the children move about to their tasks and the spontaneous way in which they talk to visitors make a marked impression. In classroom or laboratory or shop, it is usual to find about as much whispering as in a concert audience, with the same motives, freed of "rules of order," for quiet. A natural atmosphere of orderly and tolerant conduct seems to be formed in such a school.

The writer witnessed an interesting study in spontaneous discipline in one of the Saturday voluntary classes at the Froebel School. The wood-working shop was filled with little boys who were fussing over the scraps left by the week's work and trying to make toys and knick-knacks out of them. The teacher was in the room, but was exercising no control over the children. Yet each little boy worked on his own little job as indefatigably as if he were under a drill-master. If any of them became weary and was moved to interfere with another small worker, he was apt to be brushed off as if he were an irritating fly. The theory at the back of such freedom is that rules in the school tempt to infraction, and school discipline is, as a result, largely an attempt to solve problems which the rules directly manufacture. Some visitors, appalled by the freedom of the Gary schools, look about for signs of depredation. But they do not seem to find any. The visitor gets the impression that these schools have acquired a "public sense." The schools are the children's own institution, and are public in the same broad sense that streets and parks are public. The tone is of a glorified democratic club, where members are availing themselves of privileges which they know are theirs. One expects children, unless they are challenged to inventive wickedness, no more to spoil their school than a lawyer is likely to deface the panels of his club. The children seem in such a school unaffectedly to own it, and to use it as a mechanic uses his workshop or an artist his studio. The halls in the Gary school become really school streets. Benches are built by the pupils along the walls, where children are seen informally studying together. Or one comes upon a table where a boy is drawing a map, having been excused from recitation, on the theory that it is not necessary for every child to be exposed to every exercise of the class when he might do something more important outside. The children come with their parents to night school and play and run about the broad halls quite unwatched. The visitor gets the idea that children come to such a school, not because education is compulsory or because their parents send them there to get rid of them, but because what is done there is so interesting that they will not stay away. The equipment, used so freely, makes the school a substitute for the defects, not only of the poorer homes, but of the well-to-do also, in supplying activities for children.

One might say that only in a free and varied school like this was such a thing as effective discipline possible. When school activities are as attractive as they are in the Gary school, deprivation means a distinct punishment. There is ready at hand an instrument for inculcating reason into the refractory which is as powerful as the stoutest disciplinarian could wish. The ordinary school has its difficulties with discipline largely because it tries to keep up a military system of conduct without any means, now that corporal punishment is generally abolished, of punishing infractions. Marks prove ineffective, "keeping in" punishes the keeper as well as the kept, and being sent home is too often a pleasure. But in the Gary school, "being sent home" would mean being sent to a place infinitely less interesting, and being deprived of school play or any special activity would mean a real hardship. The free and spontaneous discipline of the Gary school does not mean that there is no discipline at all. Unruly cases are sometimes punished severely by the executive principal. But there is little talk about "mischievous and unruly boys." Children who, in spite of everything, are "not adapted to our kind of a school," may go to the school farm. This, however, is not a reform school for juvenile delinquents. Delicate children may be sent there for a vacation or classes go for a holiday. The farm contains a hundred acres, with a model dairy, good orchards, and substantial farm buildings. A graduate from one of the state universities is in charge, and is working to bring the farm up to a high pitch of cultivation and production. One group of boys who were there for a while, some of whom had come from homes surrounded by unwholesome conditions, others of whom wished to try farming for a livelihood, built themselves living quarters and a clubroom. They were provided with a teacher, and school work went on with the farm work. The boys received fifteen cents an hour for their work, and earned enough to pay their board and make something besides. These boys finally drifted back to the Emerson School or to work in the factories. But the farm remains as a valuable adjunct to the schools. Efforts are being made to make it a source of income and an object lesson to farmers in the vicinity.

Freedom of discipline is obtained in the Gary schools without the methods of "self-government" and "honor systems" which prevail elsewhere. Where the teachers retain all authority, such schemes can be little more than a humiliating pretense. For a time an elaborate self-government plan was tried in the Emerson School under the name of "Boyville," with a sort of parody of municipal functions. But it seems to have been too unreal to last. It has been superseded by a "students' council," elected by the pupils of the upper grades, and exercising control over athletics, social, and other student affairs. This students' council has executive charge of the "auditorium" periods, for which it elects a presiding officer and secretary, alternately a boy and a girl, every month. The elections for councilors are conducted in regular form, with ballots printed by the pupils in the school printing-shop. Booths are erected, judges appointed, and the election carried through, after a campaign, in which the parties meet, nominate a boy and girl for each office, and appoint a campaign manager who arranges a program for the campaign. The candidates make speeches, giving their views and the arguments for their policies.

Like everything in the Gary schools, this political practice is put into effect on a broader scale. During a recent campaign the students' council in the Emerson School arranged a public meeting at which prominent men of the city appeared and argued for their respective parties. The meeting was entirely organized and managed by the pupils. Such practical application seems far more real and instructive than the usual play at self-government.

Student organization in the Gary schools grows out of real work. Athletic teams and sports of various kinds are connected directly with the gymnasium work and organized play. Glee clubs and orchestras grow out of the music work. A monthly paper is conducted by the high-school pupils as part of their English work, and printed by them in the school printing-shop. There are, strictly speaking, no "extra-curricular activities" in the Gary schools. The curriculum deliberately provides for all wholesome activities, and the student interests grow out of it. Problems of "fraternities" and of the control of school athletics, which confront so many schools, are thus avoided. The students do not get into the habit of thinking of their clubs and teams as something outside of the school community life.

An example of how spontaneous organization may spring up is that of the boys' ninth-grade English class last year in the Emerson School, which formed itself into the Emerson Improvement Association. It tries to suggest civic improvements for the school community, and the speaking and writing necessary to the conducting of the affairs of the organization provide the basis for the English work.

This illustrates the way that effort is made to take advantage of all the spontaneity and initiative which pupils display in organization. The moral effects of this active form of education are clearly great. Professor Dewey thinks it is a mistake to consider that an interesting and free school "makes things too easy for the child." In the ideal school the interests and needs of the child are identical. It is a mistake, he says, to think that interesting things are necessarily easy. They may be hard, but the interest overcomes the difficulty, and it is in the overcoming that the moral value lies. Irksome tasks may be valuable, but it is not in their irksomeness that their value lies. Work that appeals to pupils as worth while, that holds out the promise of resulting in something to their own or the school's interests, involves just as much persistence and concentration as work given by the sternest advocate of disciplinary drill.

DRAWING FROM A MODEL AT THE EMERSON SCHOOL

Notice frieze on wall designed and painted by the children themselves

Most of the visitors to the Gary schools bear witness to the excellent tone of the pupils, "the free and natural way," to quote one authoritative teacher, "in which pupils govern themselves without the rigorous discipline found in other systems." Dr. Harlan Updegraff, of the Federal Bureau of Education, says, "The pupils of the Gary schools seem to display greater self-control, more self-respect, and more thoughtful consideration for others than the pupils of the same age in most of the better school systems of to-day. I am inclined to think that it comes largely from their games and play, but a part of it is due to the organization of the school, and to the practices that have evolved in its administration. No child in Gary has a single teacher who is the object of his hero-worship, upon whom he tends to become more or less dependent, or his arch-enemy whom he detests with a growing hatred. The Gary pupil has several teachers, each of whom affects him in a different way. He becomes more conscious of his individuality in this way, and learns to determine for himself what he should do and become. Under such a system the influence of fellow pupils becomes relatively stronger than in the ordinary school. It is, therefore, highly important that care be taken to further the development of right ideals in the student body. Organized play has its great value here. Self-control, coöperation, courage, self-respect, consideration for others, and a sense of justice have been developed in the Gary youth to a noticeable degree, largely, it seems to me, through the spirit that prevails in consequence of the administration of the physical training department. Pupils who love their school better than the streets, who have a good physical tone through their play and physical exercises, and who have good self-control and independence of thought, must naturally have a more favorable attitude toward school work."

Such a school will evidently train character as a by-product. Self-activity, self or coöperative instruction, freedom of movement, *camaraderie* with teachers, interesting and varied work, study, and play, a sense of what the school is doing, social introspection, — all combine to give an admirable moral training and to produce those desirable intellectual and moral qualities that the world most needs to-day. Not obedience but self-reliance does such a school cultivate.

VIII

CRITICISMS AND EVALUATIONS

The criticisms directed against the Gary schools by superintendents and teachers are criticisms rather of the whole educational philosophy behind the institution than objections to the detailed working-out of the philosophy. Those who follow Professor Dewey's philosophy find in the Gary schools — as Professor Dewey does himself — the most complete and admirable application yet attempted, a synthesis of the best aspects of the progressive "schools of to-morrow."

Concrete criticisms almost all concern the alleged additional burdens laid upon the public, the teacher, and the pupil. As far as the public goes, the fact has been brought out that the Gary school is actually a cheaper kind of a school than is the ordinary public school, even when run in the most economical and scientific manner. The charge that the Gary schools are aided by private corporation enterprise has already been discussed.

The facts are, of course, that the schools are all supported in the usual way, by local and state appropriations. The city of Gary is not overtaxed to support its schools, neither does the United States Steel Corporation pay more than its proportionate share of the local taxes. Nor is there any truth in the impression that the operation of the Gary plan is confined to the two larger school plants of the city. Although these two plants accommodate three quarters of the children of the city, the Gary plan is in operation in all the schools. In the two larger schools, Emerson and Froebel, the academic work extends from the kindergarten through all twelve grades. In the other schools there are no high-school students. Four of the other schools have eight grades, one has six, one is only for children in the kindergarten and first two grades. These schools have no high-school department because they are too small and the schools with high-school departments are easily accessible. All the schools have real shopwork, though in not all of them is the apprentice-repair feature possible. All the schools have play and recreation facilities. The smaller schools lack swimming-pools, but the children use the well-equipped Y.M.C.A. All the schools have "auditorium," science, music, and expression work. All the schools either contain a branch of the public library or else use the main building near by. All the schools have an eight-hour day.

The charge that the Gary schools are too costly for imitation cannot be sustained. We have seen the ingenious efforts of the various features of the Gary plans to reduce costs, and there is a wealth of figures to show in detail the greater economy of the Gary plan. Superintendent Wirt has made an estimate that for an outlay of $6,000,000, "part-time" could be wholly abolished in the New York City public schools by an adoption of the Gary plan. The requisition of the board of superintendents in 1914 was for an appropriation of $40,000,000, simply for new buildings, which would require large sums for operation and maintenance and lack the equipments of the Gary plan. By the multiple use of facilities, Superintendent Wirt has shown that the number of school plants in New York could actually be reduced and yet the part-time of 132,000 children abolished. At the same time that this was done, the school day would actually be increased and the facilities more than doubled. A comparison between the *per-capita* costs of instruction in the Gary and New York City schools, figured in average daily attendance for 1913–14, has been made by Mrs. Alice Barrows-Fernandez. (The Jefferson School in Gary is used for the comparison because it is more like the elementary schools in New York than any other school in Gary.)

Pupil per-capita cost for Jefferson School, Gary, including instruction and supplies	$31.72
Pupil per-capita cost for elementary schools in New York City, including instruction and supplies	40.24
Pupil per-capita cost for the two Gary schools which have kindergarten, elementary school, and full vocational shops —	
Emerson, with one third of the school high-school pupils	56.12
Froebel, with twelve per cent high-school pupils	32.85
Pupil per-capita cost in New York City —	
Elementary schools	40.24
High schools	104.74
Vocational schools for boys	86.48
Vocational schools for girls	142.32

"In other words," says Mrs. Barrows-Fernandez in her report, "in the Froebel School, which is typical of the average school because only twelve per cent of its pupils are in high school, twelve years in elementary school and high school costs the city for one pupil twelve times $32.85, or $394.20. In New York, eight years in elementary school costs the city for one student eight times $40.24, or $329.92, and four years in high school costs four times $104.74, or $418.96; or for the twelve years, $748.88. In Gary for the $394.20, a student could also get more vocational training than is given in a separate trade school. The New York boy would get none of this in the elementary school. Even if we make allowances for the fact that the average salary of teachers in elementary schools and high schools in New York City is one third higher than in Gary, it is obvious that the balance of economy is immensely in favor of Gary as against a large typical city school system operated on the conventional lines."

It seems established that the Gary plan imposes no burdens upon the public, either in Gary or in the communities who imitate the plan, but rather provides increased facilities at reduced cost, besides immense facilities for adults. As for the burden upon the teacher, much has been said to the effect that the Gary plan is unpopular among teachers because of the extra work it entails. In connection with this criticism, it must be remembered that the Gary plan postulates an educational philosophy different from that of the ordinary public schools. Teachers trained in schools managed with rigid administrative and disciplinary methods naturally find adjustment difficult in a system which repeatedly calls upon them for initiative, alters their relations to their pupils, and requires a more practical attitude of "application" toward the subject-matter of instruction. Experience seems to show that many teachers who at first found this adjustment burdensome have later come to prefer the Gary plan. One teacher with a fine scholastic training, who had taught for many years under the traditional form of organization, is quoted by Dean Burris as saying, "I did not like it when I came here a year ago, but I begin to like it and see what it is all about, so I am going to stay."

This attitude would seem to be typical of the intelligent teacher who comes to appreciate what it is all about and the valuable educational advantages which the system provides for the teacher herself. And although the problem of securing teachers has been somewhat difficult in Gary, owing to the newness of the town, the large factory population, and the relative absence of organized social life, most visitors are impressed by the unusual personal caliber of the head teachers.

It is difficult to see where the Gary plan involves extra burdens for teachers. The teaching period is only four hours a day, with an hour for "auditorium" and an hour for "application." This is certainly no more exacting than the five-hour teaching day of the ordinary teacher. All "home work" and "paper work," moreover, is supposed to be done by the Gary teacher during school hours, so that her school day is over when the bell rings. This makes her real school day actually shorter than that of the teacher in the ordinary school, whose afternoons and evenings must often be spent in correcting papers, etc. The Gary teacher is supposed to have leisure and to behave in school and out of school as a good citizen actively interested in the community welfare. The Saturday school work, for which the teachers are called upon in turn, is paid for at a rate of one dollar an hour. The care and work involved in the "register-teacher" plan is certainly offset by its valuable educational value for the teacher herself.

It should be clear that the various features of the Gary plan tend to relieve the teacher of burdens and particularly of nervous strain. The teaching of special subjects by special teachers relieves the grade teacher of the obligation of teaching, under the exacting direction of supervisors, subjects like music and drawing with which she may be little acquainted. The departmentalizing of subjects down through the lower grades gives a breadth to the teachers' work, and enables them to concentrate on the subjects which interest them, rather than diffuse their attention among many. The absence of uniform standards, the absence of formal term examinations for which a whole class must be prepared, the promotion of children by subjects rather than whole classes, as well as the division of grades according to rate of progress, — all this makes for a great saving in the teacher's nervous energy. She does not have the strain of passing her whole class in every subject, of finishing her course on schedule time, of cramming for examinations. She has some freedom in the division of her time and a voice in the making of the course and curriculum. The less experienced teacher has in her classroom the assistance and advice of the senior teacher, as well as of the head teacher of her subjects in the head school. Teachers are not rivals, but colleagues as in a college faculty.

The freer methods of discipline are much to the teacher's advantage. When the ideal is no longer to keep the classroom in a rigid military silence, a large part of the teacher's energy may go into teaching which formerly went into the maintenance of discipline. Where "interest" and "application" and "learning by doing" are the keynotes, and where every one — teacher and pupil alike — is at some time in the course both teaching some one and learning from some one, the teacher is no longer interested in "making the child obey," or "commanding his respect." No official gulf is set between teachers and pupils. It is discipline that wears out most teachers, — and children too, — and a greater flexibility makes for the lessening of nervous strain on both.

The custom of "helpers and observers," the emphasis on discussion rather than formal recitation, even take a certain amount of actual teaching out of the hands of the teachers. The teacher, as in the Montessori method, becomes the guide and mentor rather than direct preceptor. She is no longer so much concerned with predigesting subject-matter and presenting it in logical form to the pupil, only to draw it from him again in recitation and written examination. She is rather concerned with directing the large amount of practical work which the Gary child does in every course, and in devising methods of "application," or in turning the work into practical value for the school community. Those classes where the "helper and observer" system obtains are, to a large degree, self-instructing. The older child tells the younger what he is doing in shop or laboratory, etc., and when the younger child comes to take up the work, he is already familiar with materials and apparatus and the significance of the course. Raw new classes thus do not have to be constantly broken in by the teacher. This means a very large saving of labor for the teacher, while it makes for the more thorough understanding on the part of the pupil. In the physical education work and in the organized play, the older pupils are enlisted as assistants to the teachers. Superintendent Wirt's new plans involve the employment throughout the different departments as teachers' assistants of a class of older pupils, selected for their interest and ability. Such work not only gives the student the best possible training for developing leadership, initiative, and the ability to assume responsibility, but it also relieves the teachers and makes possible many small classes without extra teachers and without extra rooms.

From the teachers' point of view, then, the numerous ways in which the Gary plan relieves the nervous strain and actual responsibility of teaching, and removes the pressure of outside work, more than compensate for the slightly longer actual time during which the teacher must be in the school plant. And since this longer time means increased salary, it is clear that the teacher under the Gary plan is the gainer in every direction.

The criticisms of the Gary plan on the ground that the long school day and varied curriculum overload the pupil can scarcely be sustained in view of the fact that the "school day" is not merely a lengthening of the ordinary public school day, but an absorbing, in healthful activities of play, exercise and manual work, of time which would otherwise be spent in demoralizing street and alley or in idleness at home. We have seen that this additional activity is not gained at the expense of the academic studies, but comes from giving the children interesting things to do in the surplus hours in which they are usually left to take care of themselves. The freedom of the Gary schools, and the constant passing back and forth between school and home, church, etc., does not seem to make for truancy. The percentage of attendance in November, 1914, was for boys 92.9, for girls, 91.6, — a remarkable record when it is considered that boy truancy in most city schools is much the greater. For the year 1913–14 the percentage of attendance was for boys 89.5, for girls, 89.2.

The criticism of the Gary school on the ground that the shopwork either involves the risk of exploiting the pupil, or else introduces him to manual activity at too early an age, ignores the fact that the manual work is really unspecialized and is introduced so gradually into the child's life that it is scarcely felt as work. "Play" and "work" are merged in "interesting activity," and almost unconsciously the child finds himself absorbed in work which may be his vocation later on. Whether it is to be his vocation or not, the Gary school believes that such work is a good thing in the education of all children. Many educators believe that the novel form of shopwork in the Gary school offers a solution for the problems of industrial training. There is great risk, in schools where shopwork is introduced apart from the academic work, as in special technical high schools, of an undemocratic and invidious distinction between the manual worker and the brain worker. In plans of organization, such as the Ettinger plan in New York City, with a preliminary course of "prevocational training," in which the prospective industrial pupil in the seventh and eighth grades discovers by hasty experimentation which trade his aptitudes fit him to pursue, there is great danger that the vocational work will be left unassimilated to the rest of the school work and the child trained into a narrow specialist. Such "vocational training" deserves all the criticism that has been directed against it by the opponents of a too "utilitarian" education. The Gary type of vocational training keeps the industrial work constantly in touch with the other activities, and makes it a really "cultural" branch of the school community work. And because the children lay their foundations of skill and interest so early and work at real work under real workmen, their training from a practical point of view is as good as, if not better than, the special trade school is likely to give them. More shops are actually supported in the Gary school than even the most elaborate special trade school can afford to provide. The correlation of day courses with evening continuation courses, the great attention to science, the emphasis on the social and communal bearing of all activities, — all this means a higher type of vocational training than has been worked out generally in the public school. If he is intelligent, he will be better qualified for skilled work than the more narrowly trained worker. "This is the age," says Superintendent Wirt, "of the engineer, of machinery, and of big business. The school business enterprises offer a type of industrial and commercial education facilities . . . adapted to modern industry and business. There are big business problems and machinery problems in the school." These problems evolved in the life of a school community give an education, he holds, superior to what can be given even in schools narrowly devoted to shop-training. And it can give the training in small groups or even to individuals, where the special school has to give instruction in large classes to make it pay at all. As Mrs. Barrows-Fernandez puts it, "If you believe that vocational education is confined to specific training for a trade, and that this must be carried on in a separate trade school, and that general education has no relation to it except as it may add a fringe of culture, then you will think that there is no vocational education in Gary. But, on the other hand, if you belong to the group that believes that what children under sixteen need in the way of vocational work is not specialized trade training on top of an inadequate elementary-school education, but fundamental industrial training closely related to the science and academic work, and made real and natural because it is one of the many activities of the whole school, — then you will come away from Gary feeling that the vocational work there represents the soundest point of view and the best practical accomplishment in vocational work for children under sixteen that can be found anywhere in the country."

In New York City, where an extended experimentation is being carried on with the Gary plan, considerable controversy is said to have arisen over the provision of the Gary scheme which permits outside institutions, including churches, to coöperate with the school and take children for a few hours a week for any special work, amusement, or instruction which the schools cannot give. The fear was expressed there that this provision would mean the entering wedge of religion into the public school.

As outlined by Mr. Wirt, however, the Gary plan holds no brief for religious instruction. It has no concern with any church activity as such. What it tries to do is to coördinate the community child-welfare agencies with the school. The lengthening of the school day absorbs an hour which would otherwise be spent by the city child in the street, or at home, church, or settlement. All the Gary school does is to organize and systematize this hour. It may be spent by the child either in play or auditorium at the school, or in any outside activity which provides wholesome activities for children. The object is to coördinate the community opportunities so that they may function regularly and vitally instead of spasmodically as at present. The school gives to all the agencies which pretend to be interested in the child's welfare a chance to spend themselves effectively. It brings up to the level of public discussion, for the first time, the question what sort of home, church, and neighborhood activities are good for children.

Into this scheme the church enters merely as a community institution. As long as any considerable number of the parents of the children in a school believe that religious instruction is valuable, no public school which attempts to be really public can refuse to release children for this purpose, just as it releases them for playgrounds, settlements, libraries, home music, or other instruction. This outside time is not taken from study. Nor are the children turned out into the streets to be taken care of by the churches and other institutions. No child is excused unless the parents make formal application. If the parents do not do this, the child stays at the school for the full seven or eight hours of work, study, and play. The burden of responsibility rests entirely upon the parents and the churches. The teachers have nothing to do with the matter, either in segregating the children or seeing where they go. There seems to be little fear that the practice will not conform to the theory. Mr. Wirt tells us that his work-study-and-play school had been functioning for twelve years in Bluffton and Gary before any religious organization took advantage of this provision. The idea that the opportunity would unduly increase religious influence in the schools seems to be groundless. In the Jefferson School in Gary, which has been longest in operation under the Wirt plan, and where the fullest efforts have been made by all the sects and religions of the town to provide this supplementary instruction, scarcely half the children in the spring of 1915 were going out to any sort of religious training whatever. And in one of the Wirt schools in New York, where unusual efforts have been made by some of the churches to meet the new plan, not even half of the children are released for this purpose. In another Wirt school in New York, none of the children are released, because there is no demand for it on the part of the parents.

What the Gary plan seems to do is not to bring religion into the schools, but for the first time to take it out of the schools. The relations now between church and school are hidden. The Gary plan brings them out into the open. The establishment of a fair, free, and open relation between the school and all other community institutions is of utmost importance. No institution which has anything valuable to offer the child will lose by such a relation. No outside power can dominate or even partially control a public school which has established it.

We may sum up the Gary school, then, as primarily a school community for children of all ages between nursery and college, providing wholesome activities under a fourfold division of work, study, play, and expression. It aims to provide the best possible environment for the growing child throughout the course of a full eight-hour day. The school community, replacing the old-time education of household and school, aims to be as self-sustaining as possible, all activities contributing to the welfare of the school community life. By the multiple use of school facilities, on the plan of public-service principles, such a school may be provided at no more expense than that of the ordinary public school. The economics effected by this multiple use enable the Gary school to provide recreational and educational facilities for adults as well as children all the year round, as well as to pay better salaries to teachers, and completely solve "part-time problems." It makes the school the cultural center of a community with parks, libraries, and museums functioning as contributory to the school, as well as all other activities which provide wholesome interests for children. It makes the school, for the first time, a genuine "social center," and a genuinely "public school" in a comprehensive sense scarcely realized hitherto.

No better evaluation of the Gary plan has been made than that by William Paxton Burris, Dean of the College for Teachers, University of Cincinnati, in the *Bulletin* of the United States Bureau of Education, 1914, no. 18. In his opinion the school system at Gary provides: —

"1. For the better use of school-buildings day and evening, including Saturdays, the year round, making it possible to save large sums of money expended for this purpose."

This multiple use of school plants, which secures greatly increased facilities at greatly reduced cost, while it permits the giving of full-time instruction to all the children of even the congested school districts, is the aspect which has appealed most generally to educators outside of Gary. For administrators confronted with problems of part-time, it makes an examination of the Wirt plan almost essential. No educationist can afford to ignore a plan which, in mere details of mechanical administration, provides not only a full-time program, but actually a longer school day, for all the children in the city school — something hitherto considered impossible in the larger school systems. The Gary plan seems to provide an easy solution for these difficulties which grow progressively worse in the large city with every year.

"2. The possibility of a better division of

time between the old and the new studies, the 'regular studies' and 'special activities.' "

The Gary plan provides not only an enriched curriculum, but an unusually favorable and harmonious balance between the various activities. The larger emphasis on science and manual work has not made the school ultra-utilitarian in its purpose. The Gary schools have not been "turned into mills and factories," as certain educators have feared. For many visitors, the Gary school is a living refutation of the idea that the useful and the beautiful are opposed. The new school plants, such as the Emerson and Froebel, are spacious and dignified buildings, with many touches of thoughtful taste that one usually associates only with the high schools of exceptionally wealthy and cultivated suburban communities. The presence of pictures, the cultivation of music, the emphasis on expression, the teaching of literature, the systematic use of the public library, indicate a determined effort to bring the cultural aspects of education to the front, and make them as real a part of the school life as the more striking special activities. The "application" work involves constant care and interest in the enhancement of the beauty of the school plant. The actual charm of the school life in Gary — the conservatories and gardens, the play, the freedom of the children, the dramatic expression, the absence of strain and confusion, the happiness of the children — is testified to by most visitors. A very beautiful school life seems to be lived, paradoxical as it may seem, where every activity is motivated by application and expression, where the learning is by doing and not by mere studying.

"3. Greater flexibility in adapting studies to exceptional children of all kinds, thereby diminishing the necessity of special schools."

The Gary plan provides a school which is adapted to almost every kind of a child. It does not try to adapt the child to the school, casting off automatically those who do not fit. But it adapts the school to the very unequal needs and capacities of the children. Such a school seems to be one where capacities will be developed wherever there are capacities, a school where something like equal educational opportunity can be given, as it cannot be in the ordinary public school. It can almost be said that the only reason for keeping a child home from the Gary school would be a case of contagious disease. If the child is physically weak, so that he cannot undertake all the work, he may take what he can and use the other facilities of the school as one would use a sanitarium for regaining health. The daily program permits a child to spend all his time in the special activities if this is best for him. He may spend his time resting in the open air, or in supervised play until he gains strength to do the regular work. The defective child may work at what he can in the way of manual activity. And the retarded child may take such activities as will awaken his interest, and gradually bring him up to the level of his grade. An elementary school system like this has no need for the expensive special open-air schools, classes for defectives, etc., special trade schools or commercial schools. In the organized life of the complete school community, the child may find approximately what he needs.

"4. The possibility of more expert teaching through the extension of the departmental plan of organization."

"5. The better use of playtime, thereby preventing influences which undo the work of the schools."

"6. More realism in vocational and industrial work, by placing it under the direction of expert workmen from the ranks of laboring men, selected for their personal qualities and teaching ability as well as their skill in the trade industries."

The organization of the industrial and other vocational work offers many practical advantages to the young worker. Not only does he have the evening continuation courses and the privilege of coming back to the school shops in the daytime when unemployed, but the most practical foundation is laid for the development of coöperative courses between school and factory on the lines of the well-known Fitchburg plan. The flexibility of administration and curriculum in the Gary school allows him to attend the academic class during slack hours, or to divide the job and the school with another student. The Gary school even offers to provide special instruction for part-time students for any desired number of hours a week, or allows them to work on their own initiative. In 1914 in Gary there were said to be about one hundred part-time students. The plan of the all-year school also offers peculiar opportunities to the young worker. The opportunity of finding employment is increased fourfold. For instead of throwing all the pupils on the market to find jobs at the same time, one quarter of those who needed work would be available throughout the year. Instead of one continuous apprentice in an industry or trade, therefore, four pupils could take his place in alternation. Instead of one young workman spending all his time at work and none at school, four would be getting a full schooling of thirty-six weeks in the year, and twelve weeks of practical apprentice training in the factory. Thus the Gary plan makes it easy for the young worker to get the maximum benefit of the modern school and his apprenticeship at the same time.

A word should be said about the value of the vocational industrial training that the Gary school gives, from the point of view of

THE FOUNDRY AT THE EMERSON SCHOOL

Notice group of curious children at window

preparation for efficiency in the industrial world. The organization of the manual work as a part of the regular curriculum prevents the narrow specialization of the trade school. It tends to turn the young worker out, not as a part of the industrial machine fitted to do only one thing, but equipped to meet a dynamic, rapidly changing industrial world which demands above all things versatility, and which scraps methods and machines as ruthlessly as it does men. Only the man of rounded training and resourcefulness who can turn his hand quickly to a variety of occupations has a chance to-day to rise above the mass. The tendency of the old public school, in spite of its fancied "liberal" curriculum, was to turn out only very low-grade specialists in book-learning. The student who comes from the well-rounded curriculum of the Gary school into the industrial world is bound to be more alert, more interested in, and more cognizant of, what he is doing. The Gary school seems to be making an effort to produce the type of mind perhaps the most needed to-day, that of the versatile engineer, the mind that adapts and masters mechanism. This exactness, resourcefulness, inventiveness, pragmatic judgment of a machine by its product, the sense of machinery as a means not an end in itself, — these qualities of mind which come from an emphasis on applied science are the qualities which society demands in almost every industry, profession, and trade. The Gary school tends to cultivate this type of intelligence. For this type of mind, "culture" would not be a fringe, but a more or less integral part of life, because it had been woven in from the earliest years in the school community. On the other hand, skilled labor would not seem degrading or of lower value, for it too would have had its equal part in the school life.

"7. Better facilities for the promotion of the health of children."

The large amount of play, the spacious and sanitary school plants, the care of the special school physicians and school nurses who devote their whole time to the purpose, insure the needed attention to the physical well-being of the children.

"8. The possibility of having pupils do work in more than one grade and of promoting them by subjects instead of by grades."

"9. The possibility of having pupils help each other."

The "helper and observer" system, applied not only in the relations between children, but between teachers, and between teachers inside the school and visitors, is one of the most valuable features of the Gary plan. It entirely alters the usual relations, making for a coöperative instead of a competitive spirit in work, and facilitating enormously the work of both pupils and teachers. Children learn by watching and asking questions — "picking up" — in the most natural way in the world, in contrast to the formal and stilted ways of the traditional classroom work.

"10. An organization which prevents a chasm between the elementary and high school, and prevents dropping out of school at critical periods in the lives of pupils by the introduction, at such times, of subjects which appeal to awakening interests not satisfied by a continuous and exclusive devotion to the 'common branches.' "

The Gary plan, which includes all the grades in one school plant wherever possible, prevents these chasms more successfully than even such schemes as the junior high school which are being extensively experimented with elsewhere. The Gary school has an extraordinary hold on its pupils. There is no incentive for leaving school, since the school provides for the needs of the most diversely equipped children, gives them the practical vocational training they may want, and even allows their working part-time while continuing with the school. All those problems of "pupil-mortality," whereby half the children in our public schools are said never to pass beyond the sixth grade, are almost automatically avoided in a school which deliberately sets itself to meeting the individual child's needs. The success of the Gary school in holding its pupils is indicated in the fact that, in spite of the short time the Gary schools have been in existence, the proportion of high-school pupils in Gary is said to be almost twice as large as that in the schools of New York City.

"11. A saving in the cost of instruction by

reducing overhead charges for supervisors, making it possible to pay better salaries or reduce the number of pupils per teacher, or both."

"12. A plan which brings together, in a unitary way, with economy and efficiency in management, the other recreational and educational agencies of the city."

These evaluations of Dean Burris's sum up the various aspects of the Gary plan as it appeals to practical educators. It must be remembered that the Gary school represents not a rigid system, or a static and completed mechanism. Its chief value is that it provides a flexible program and facility for change and development. Any examples of details in the curricula or details of administration can only be tentative, for it is an experimental school, where every one is constantly studying and learning. It is a growing organism. The only limit to its growth seems to lie in the imagination of teachers and pupils. Even when it starts with an admirable equipment, its life is only begun. It is the use of the equipment, the constant appeal to the imagination and to expression that is the real education. In such a school, the cultivation of resource may go on indefinitely. Such a school provides that "embryonic community life" which Professor Dewey expresses as his ideal of a school, where in actual work the child senses the occupations and interests of the larger world into which he is some time actively to enter.

We may say, then, that the Gary school has national significance because it is the first public school system in successful established operation which has been able to solve the pressing and apparently insoluble problems of the city school; which has kept pace with changing industrial and social conditions, and adapts the school to every kind of a child; which synthesizes the best educational endeavors of the day, and provides the facilities which educators have vainly sought to provide for all the children, but have only succeeded in providing at great expense for the more advanced and older pupils of the community; which marks a distinct advance in democratic education; which realizes the ideal of a truly public school, in providing for all the people all of the time; and, which, in its simple organization and ingenious financial economies, furnishes a practical working-model for imitation and adaptation in other communities, large and small.

APPENDIX

I

DISTRIBUTION OF EXPENDITURES

August 1, 1914 — July 31, 1915

Schools of Gary, Indiana

REGULAR SCHOOL (TEN MONTHS, FIVE DAYS PER WEEK, EIGHT-HOUR DAY)

Largest Three Schools with No. of Pupils	*Emerson School (895)*	*Froebel (1847)*	*Jefferson (764)*	*All schools (4789)*
Instruction—				
Salaries of supervisors and principals, and miscellaneous	$2,750.19	$4,189.95	$2,016.60	$13,745.75
Salaries of teachers	27,954.77	46,373.36	16,713.70	113,533.24
Supplies............	854.66	758.58	367.00	2,660.09
Total cost of instruction......	$31,559.62	$51,321.89	$19,097.30	$129,939.08
Operation and maintenance —				
Janitors' wages......	$3,908.80	$4,936.02	$1,131.11	$12,203.15
Fuel, water, light, supplies...........	4,815.03	5,234.70	1,205.11	13,799.49
Total cost of operation.........	$8,723.83	$10,170.72	$2,336.22	$26,002.62
Maintenance	7,420.40	6,050.67	7,418.36*	26,574.62

* Includes new heating plant.

SATURDAY SCHOOL (TEN MONTHS, EIGHT-HOUR DAY)

Schools	*Emerson*	*Froebel*	*Jefferson*	*All schools*
Instruction............	$1,782.20	$2,721.57	$860.28	$6,909.52
Operation	1,713.63	1,690.83	344.65	4,332.31

SUMMER SCHOOL (TWO MONTHS)

Schools	*Emerson*	*Froebel*	*Jefferson*	*All schools*
Instruction —				
Salaries of supervisors and principals	$831.56	$1,349.65	$543.75	$3,375.20
Salaries of teachers.	4,213.63	3,678.08	779.58	10,602.91
Supplies............	38.61	33.30	30.50	114.31
Total cost of instruction	$5,083.80	$5,061.03	$1,353.83	$14,092.42
Operation —				
Janitors' wages......	$1,317.98	$1,542.37	$251.03	$3,424.34
Fuel, etc............	794.37	1,308.42	131.25	2,421.95
Total cost of operation.........	$2,112.35	$2,850.79	$382.28	$5,846.29
Maintenance	1,149.41	689.79	1,682.55	4,165.90

SUNDAY SCHOOL (TWO PLANTS, FOUR HOURS WEEKLY)

Schools	*Emerson*	*Froebel*	*All schools*
Salaries of teachers	$103.00	$128.00	$231.00
Operation..........................	954.56	847.60	1,802.16

EVENING SCHOOL (FIVE EVENINGS WEEKLY OF TWO HOURS EACH, NINE MONTHS OF SCHOOL)

Schools	*Emerson*	*Froebel*	*All schools*
Salaries of supervisors and principals..............................	$1,091.07	$1,731.45	$3,813.24
Salaries of teachers...............	5,112.89	5,828.00	13,675.73
Supplies	340.54	471.68	1,042.84
Total cost of instruction....	$6,544.50	$8,031.13	$18,531.81
Operation....................	2,283.91	2,392.68	5,872.55

PUPIL *PER-CAPITA* YEAR (TWELVE MONTHS; ALL ACTIVITIES)

Schools	*Emerson*	*Froebel*	*Jefferson*	*All schools*
Per-capita cost for				
Instruction	$35.26	$27.79	$25.00	$27.13
Operation	9.75	5.50	3.06	5.43
Maintenance	8.29	3.27	9.71	5.55
Current cost, total	$53.30	$36.56	$37.77	$38.11
Permanent improvements	11.43	7.81	14.43	10.88
Grand total	$64.73	$44.37	$52.20	$48.99
General control	—	—	—	3.54
Other payments	—	—	—	7.75
Auxiliary agency	—	—	—	1.02

ENROLLMENT

Day school	*Enrollment*	*Average daily attendance*	*No. of teachers*	*Average salary*	*Enrollment per teacher*
Emerson	895	769.80	31	$915.78	27.56
Froebel	1,847	1,591.06	57	813.56	31.50
Jefferson	764	661.70	22	759.71	33.50
All schools	4,789	4,043.98	142	802.59	33.70
Summer schools	1,700				
Evening schools	182,348*				

* Number of student hours

TOTAL EXPENDITURES — TWELVE MONTHS — ALL ACTIVITIES (REGULAR, SATURDAY, SUNDAY, SUMMER, EVENING SCHOOLS

Instruction	$169,703.83
Operation	43,855.93
Maintenance	30,740.52
Total current cost	244,300.28
Total expenditures	$362,325.73

II

SUPERINTENDENT WIRT'S REPORT

ON THE

REORGANIZATION OF THE BRONX SCHOOLS, NEW YORK CITY

Showing how the Gary Plan may be adapted to the Usual School Plant

THESE twelve schools, I am informed, are the most congested of any group of twelve schools in New York City. There are only 25,331 sittings in these schools and 35,580 children were registered December 31, 1914, — 10,249 more than sittings. The registration is 140 per cent of the sittings. But 2500 of the present sittings, representing 50 classrooms, are unsatisfactory. There are 779 classes in the schools and only 480 satisfactory classrooms. The classes are 162 per cent of the satisfactory classrooms.

Two new schools are under construction, and a leased school-building of fifteen classrooms is nearing completion. These three buildings will provide accommodations for 4500 children and 103 additional classes. When these three buildings are completed, there will be 583 satisfactory classrooms for 779 classes. The registration of the twelve schools increased 4000 pupils from December 31, 1913, to December 31, 1914. At the present rate of increase the new buildings will not take care of the increase in school attendance during the construction of the said buildings. Four new buildings in addition to those under construction are needed now to give each child attending the schools a satisfactory school seat. Because of financial limitations the Board of Education is asking for only six new elementary-school buildings for the entire city, and *two* of the six, *to cost approximately $1,000,000*, are proposed for the relief of the twelve schools named. If the two additional schools requested, together with the three under construction, could be made ready for use to-morrow, there would still be 4000 children without satisfactory seats and no provision for normal growth in the immediate future.

I herewith submit a plan for the reorganization of the twelve schools named, so that 1022 classes may be satisfactorily accommodated in place of the 583 now provided for.

Under the New Organization unsatisfactory annexes are vacated, and unsatisfactory classrooms are used for auditorium, playrooms, laboratories, and workshops. In place of the 779 classes and 35,580 children now in the schools, room will be secured for 242 additional classes and a total registration of 46,000 children. A future increase in school registration of approximately 10,000 children will thus be provided for.

To accomplish this reorganization, rather extensive annexes are necessary at four schools, costing approximately $475,000. The remaining eight schools need only slight structural changes and additional equipment, costing approximately $44,500. Additional land should be purchased for four of the schools, costing approximately

$225,000 [a total of $744,500 for twelve schools, as against $1,000,000 for two new plants on the old plan].

The cost of the four annexes, the remodeling, the equipment, and the additional land will be much less than the cost for buildings, equipment, and sites for the proposed two new schools. If the proposed two-new-schools plan is followed, a total satisfactory capacity on a five-hour single-school system for 671 classes will be secured, which is 108 classes short of the present enrollment. If the reorganization at less cost than the two-new-schools plan is followed, satisfactory accommodations in a longer school day will be secured for 1022 classes, which is 243 classes more than are now enrolled, — a difference of 351 classes and 16,000 children.

The true economy of the New Organization is to be found in the greater educational facilities provided for all of the children, rather than in the great capacity of the plants secured under the new plan.

The upper grades, 511 classes, will have a daily school program of the following type: 80 minutes in classroom for academic work; 40 minutes in gymnasium or play-yard or grounds for physical training and play; 40 minutes for general exercises in the auditorium; 60 minutes for luncheon; 140 minutes in classroom for academic work; and 80 minutes for drawing-rooms, science laboratories, or manual-training and workshops. The lower grades, 511 classes, will have a program of the following type: same as for upper grades, except that the last period of 80 minutes will be given to play, excursions, library, church instruction, or at home. As a rule the children will have 380 minutes in school in addition to the luncheon hour, in place of the 300 minutes provided in the regular full-time school. Such a study-work-and-play school removes the children very largely from the demoralizing life of the street, and gives ample time for academic, physical, and prevocational training.

Subjects	*Average time per week under regular full-time organization in New York City (minutes)*	*Average time per week under New Organization in Bronx schools (minutes)*
Opening exercises	75	100
Music	60	100
Physical training, recesses, physiology, hygiene	120	200
English, geography, history, and arithmetic	1010	1100
Nature-study and science	80	133
Drawing	85	133
Construction work	70	134
Total time per week	1500	1900

Under the old regular full-time organization, only manual-training and cooking-rooms are provided, and for seventh and eighth grades alone. Science laboratories for individual work, and drawing studios with special equipment, are not provided at all.

Under the New Organization, manual-training,

cooking-and sewing-shops, drawing-studios with special equipment, and science laboratories for individual work by students are provided for all the above grades. Besides, there will be sixty-three additional prevocational workshops with special equipment and teachers distributed advantageously in the twelve schools. Also there will be provided gardens, better auditoriums and music-rooms, better classrooms, gymnasiums and playgrounds.

Description of Schools

Indicating in Detail Necessary Changes to introduce Wirt Plan

Public School 28 has fifty-eight regular classes in forty-five regular classrooms, with one wood-working shop and one cooking-room. The ground floor play-yard and fine basement playroom provide ample play-space for nine classes at one time. There is a large gymnasium on the top floor that is not desirable for play, and should be used for drawing-rooms. The auditorium on the fourth floor should be made into six regular classrooms by installing permanent partitions for the sliding partitions. The wall partitions should be removed from the four combination auditorium and class-rooms on the second floor, and the auditorium thus secured should be seated for a permanent auditorium. Since four classrooms are thus used for the auditorium, there will be left only forty-one regular classrooms. Thirty-six of these should be used for regular class work. Two of the five remaining classrooms should be used for science laboratories, one for a music studio, and two for workshops. These five special rooms, with the manual-training shop and cooking-room and drawing-studios, will provide facilities for nine classes in science, drawing, music, manual-training or shopwork, at one time. Seventy-two regular classes may be accommodated in this school with thirty-six classes in thirty-six class-rooms, nine in the auditorium, nine at play, nine in special work, and nine primary classes with an extra period for play, religious instruction in churches, excursions, library work, etc.

With a full register of classes, seventy-six teachers should be employed. Fifty-six teachers should teach the history, geography, arithmetic, language, and reading, and manage the auditorium. Two teachers should have charge of the music, four of the play and physical training, one of the library, two of the drawing, two of the science laboratories, and nine of the manual training, domestic science and art, and the shopwork.

There are thirteen regular classes in the eight-room frame annex, which must be used for class purposes in order to enable the city to hold the property. A special program can be arranged for this annex, to accommodate twelve classes.

Public School 28 and the annex can therefore accommodate eighty-four classes, a gain of thirteen classes over the present enrollment, and thirty-one classes more than the normal capacity of fifty-three classes in a single-school system.

The only expense will be the placing of permanent partitions in the auditorium classrooms, and the equipment of the auditorium, laboratories, studios and shops, — approximately $10,000.

Public School 5 has twenty-seven classes in nineteen regular classrooms, a good auditorium and two portable schools. Four classes are now using the auditorium as classrooms, with only curtains for partitions. There is play space in the basement play-yard for six classes to play at once.

By removing the portable schools a satisfactory outdoor playground can be secured. The basement has a fine shoproom, large enough to accommodate two small shops. In these shops and the nineteen classrooms, with the auditorium and play facilities, thirty-two classes may be accommodated by using sixteen of the most desirable rooms for classrooms. This is five classes more than are now in the school, and thirteen more than the capacity of the main building on a five-hour single-school system.

The cost of moving the portables should be charged to the school to which they are moved. The cost for equipment and remodeling should be approximately $5,000.

Public School 32 has sixty classes in thirty-eight classrooms, with one workshop and one cooking-room. Five classrooms and one cooking-room are now in a gymnasium with only curtains for partitions. Three classrooms are unsatisfactory basement rooms, one is an unsatisfactory attic room, and twelve classrooms are combination auditorium and classrooms.

By placing permanent partitions in the combination auditoriums, twenty-nine satisfactory classrooms and five shoprooms may be secured. The gymnasium and play-yard are ample for a large school. The building is close to Bronx Park for large outdoor play-yard and for gardens. The present site can be enlarged without great cost. I believe that it is desirable to make Public School 32 a seventy-two-room school, which will enable it to accommodate twelve more classes than are now in the school.

An annex should be built containing swimming-pool, auditorium, five shops, and seven classrooms, costing approximately $100,000.

III

SUPERINTENDENT WIRT'S REPORT

ON THE

REORGANIZATION OF PUBLIC SCHOOL 89, BROOKLYN, NEW YORK.

Showing the Adaptation of the Gary Plan to the Usual School Plant

THIS school was the first to be reorganized in New York City under the Gary plan. The following quotations from Superintendent Wirt's report indicate the changes that were made in transforming a congested elementary school into a smoothly running Gary school on the duplicate plan: —

Prior to November 6, 1914, there were forty classes attending School 89. Twelve of the forty classes, representing the upper grades, were on full time, having the exclusive use of twelve of the twenty-six classrooms. The remaining twenty-eight classes were organized in groups of fourteen classes each and were accommodated in the remaining fourteen classrooms, small auditorium, and five cellar rooms, with a modification of the accompanying program. (See p. 191).

Since in this program twelve classrooms were used exclusively for twelve classes, the burden of the overcrowding was placed entirely upon the remaining fourteen classrooms. These fourteen rooms had a multiple use for eight hours a day, but the auditorium and playground were used only

School hours	*Fourteen classrooms*	*Exercises and study in auditorium and playground*
8.30– 9.30	First group — 14 classes	
9.30–10.30	First group	Second group
10.30–11.30	Second group — 14 classes	First group
11.30–12.30	Second group	First group — at lunch
12.30– 1.30	First group	Second group — at lunch
1.30– 2.30	First group	Second group
2.30– 3.30	Second group	
3.30– 4.30	Second group	

two hours a day. This means that the auditorium and playground were congested during the short time that they were in use. When it rained and all the children were required to be in the building from 9.30 to 11.30, nine classes were forced to use the five cellar rooms at one time as study-rooms. No provision was made for the systematic use of other child-welfare agencies.

The old program was not intended to secure greater facilities for children than the ordinary single-system school offers.

The principle underlying the old program was that of securing the traditional five-hour school day by supplementing the four hours in the classroom with an additional hour in playground and auditorium. Unfortunately the latter hour was used as much as possible for study in quarters that were never intended for use as a study-room and cannot be made satisfactory for study No one offers the argument that such a five-hour school is better than or even as good as five hours of regular classroom work in the ordinary single-system school.

This program was not intended to secure greater facilities for children than the ordinary single-system school offers. The purpose was to secure as nearly as possible the traditional work of the regular five-hour full-time school, and it was considered only as a temporary expedient until a sufficient number of new schools could be built to provide the regulation full-time school. Since the main object was the building of additional school-buildings for permanent relief, no funds could be expended upon this temporary double-system expedient.

In contrast to this, the new program at Public School 89 is in no sense an effort to relieve part-time by giving the children as nearly as possible a five-hour traditional school day until a new building can be built.

The sole purpose determining the new program now in use at this school is that of securing a six-hour day and much richer opportunities in a study-work-and-play school with a coördination of the activities of all child-welfare agencies.

By making the following improvements at Public School 89, the increase in capacity and additional facilities can be made permanent — a gymnasium and swimming-pool, two rooms for branch of the public library, equipment for science laboratories and auditorium, wardrobes for sixteen classes, permanent playground, and drawing- and music-studios. With the exception of the playground, the above will cost approximately $35,000.

The cost of the site and the proposed new fifty-one unit school-building, to relieve Public School 89 and two other buildings, will provide the funds for similar changes in ten schools after the plan at Public School 89. These changes would make possible a permanent increase in capacity of not less than two hundred classrooms, since in the more modern schools a less expenditure will secure greater capacity. Since a fifty-one unit building adds accommodation for only forty-eight traditional full-time classes, the satisfactory accommodation of sixteen additional classes at Public School 89 would justify the expenditure of one third the cost of the new building and site upon Public School 89, or approximately $170,000. But, as has just been pointed out, it is not necessary to spend anything like this amount.

Under the old program there were only forty classes, but one class was very large and was divided into two sections with two teachers in charge. The number of pupils attending this school is increasing rapidly, and therefore a program for forty-two classes is planned.

The forty-two classes in the New Program are divided into two duplicate schools of twenty-one classes each. In the following programs these duplicate schools are designated as the "X" School and the "Y" School.

The X School: Twenty-one of the classrooms are used for the desired academic instruction in the regular school subjects, — arithmetic, language, reading, history, and geography. The five remaining classrooms are used for the special school subjects, — science, drawing, and music. In addition to the twenty-six classrooms, the school has a manual-training shop, a domestic-science laboratory, a small auditorium, five cellar playrooms, and a kindergarten. Because the special rooms are not yet equipped (January 9, 1915), for the time being they are used for additional regular class work. Since there is no library or librarian, and since the manual-training and cooking teachers are at the building only half-time, two extra special teachers are in charge of the playground.

The X School has the following activities and facilities for carrying them on: —

Type of work	*Facilities used by each type of work*
Academic instruction..	21 classrooms.
General exercises......	Auditorium.
Play and physical training	Playground, playrooms, pool, gymnasium.
Special work	2 manual-training shops, 2 science laboratories, 2 drawing studios, 1 music studio, 1 public-library branch.

The twenty-one classes are divided into three divisions of seven classes each, as follows: —

Division 1 — seven classes, grades 6, 7, 8.
Division 2 — seven classes, grades 3, 4, 5.
Division 3 — seven classes, grades 1 and 2.

All these twenty-one classes, from the first grade to the eighth, take part in these activities according to the following program: —

School hours	*Academic instruction*	*General exercises*	*Play, etc.*	*Special*
8.30– 9.20	Arithmetic, *all divisions*			
9.20–10.10	Language, *all divisions*			
10.10–11.00		Div. 1.	Div. 3.	Div. 2.
11.00–12.00	Entire X school at luncheon			
12.00– 1.00	Reading, *all divisions*			
1.00– 1.50	History, geography, *all divisions*			
1.50– 2.40		Div. 3.	Div. 2.	Div. 1.
2.40– 3.30		Div. 2.	Div. 3.	Div. 1.
3.30– 4.30			Div. 1.	

Summary of time schedule: Pupils' time, minutes per week. (All pupils have twenty per cent more time in school.)

School department	*Division 1.*		*Division 2.*		*Division 3.*	
	X school	*N.Y. minimum*	*X school*	*N.Y. minimum*	*X school*	*N.Y. minimum*
Academic...	1050	840	1050	840	1050	880–1090
Auditorium.	250	75	250	75	250	75
Play.......	after school	80	250	150	500	180– 300
Work......	500	280	250	250	Included in academic time.	
Total......	1800	1275	1800	1315	1800	1255–1345
Full time...	1800	1500	1800	1500	1800	1200–1500

The actual time spent by the teachers according to the New Program is no longer than the established time. Each teacher has 210 minutes in regular activities, and 100 in special activities, with 20 minutes for assembling of pupils, a total of 330 minutes, which is the established time.

The two periods in special activities should be departmentalized by certain teachers giving both periods to play and physical training, and other teachers giving both periods to music, drawing, and science, etc. The manual-training teachers and the public librarian release two teachers from the work periods, who may be assigned to play and physical training. Six teachers should run the auditorium period, and the remaining teacher of the Division should be assigned to play and physical training. The only extra teachers are the manual-training teachers. If there are a few teachers who cannot do the work of the special activities successfully, they may give all of this time to regular school activities. The teachers so displaced from regular activities may give all of their time to physical training and play, music, drawing, etc.

About half of the teachers will have an extra 50-minute period in the school for grading papers, planning school work, looking after individual needs of children, or professional study. In my judgment it would be well if all teachers did their supplementary school work at the school rather than at home. Less energy will be required to do this work at the school than at home, and the public will have a better understanding of the teacher's work.

The Y School: Unfortunately the program described requires twenty-six classrooms for twenty-one classes of children in addition to the auditorium, play space, library, workshops, etc. No facility during the school day is used more than half the time by the X School. Fortunately the auditorium need be large enough to accommodate only one third of the X School. The same is true of the play space and the special work facilities. There is a great economy in using the facilities named for three periods by alternate groups, each representing one third of the school. But a higher first cost and a greater operation and maintenance cost would be justifiable in all these facilities, including the regular classrooms, if they could be used longer and accommodate more children.

Since the X School can use any of these facilities only half of the time, what objection can there be to another school of twenty-one classes using the facilities when the X School cannot use them? On p. 198 is shown a program for such a duplicate school, designated Y.

The Y School has the same time as the X School, for both pupils and teachers. Neither school could use any facility any more if the other school were not there, but both schools have better facilities every hour of the day because the other school is there. Forty-two classes of children are thus accommodated in twenty-six classrooms. Instead of building a sixteen-room additional school, with its initial cost of construction, site, janitor service, heating, maintenance, etc., an equivalent expenditure can be made for the permanent improvement and increased operating cost of the twenty-six-room school.

School hours	*Academic instruction*	*General exercises*	*Play, physical training*	*Special work*
8.30– 9.20		Div. 2.	Div. 3.	Div. 1.
9.20–10.10		Div. 3.	Div. 2.	Div. 1.
10.10–11.00	Arithmetic, *all divisions*			
11.00–12.00	Language, *all divisions*			
12.00– 1.00	Entire school at luncheon			
1.00– 1.50		Div. 1.	Div. 3.	Div. 2.
1.50– 2.40	Reading, *all divisions*			
2.40– 3.30	History, geography, *all divisions*			
3.30– 4.30			Div. 1.	

(The blank spaces represent the periods when the X School is using the facilities.)

While this program makes two schools in one possible, primarily it is planned to provide a longer school-day, i.e., six hours in place of five, and greater facilities for each child during each of the six hours. One hundred minutes' daily play is given to the primary grades, for play takes the place of work for small children. This play is gradually transformed into work, fifty minutes' work and fifty minutes' play in the intermediate grades, and one hundred minutes' work in the grammar grades, as the older children use their after-school leisure time for play. Thus the play impulse is transformed into the work impulse. Productive activities are substituted for non-productive activities. Work is made constructive play.

IV

ECONOMY OF PLAYGROUND MANAGEMENT IN GARY SCHOOL, AS CONTRASTED WITH PUBLIC PLAYGROUND

SUPERINTENDENT WIRT, at the meeting of the Department of Superintendence of the National Education Association, St. Louis, February, 1912 spoke as follows: —

We have not utilized the school plants completely unless they are used for recreation and social centers by adults. Fortunately, a school plant that provides for the constructive play and recreation activities of children is also most admirably adapted for similar activities with adults. The playground, gymnasiums, swimming-pools, auditorium, club and social rooms, library, shops, laboratories, etc., make a complete social and recreation center for adults. Experience has demonstrated that the facilities for academic instruction add also to the attractiveness of the plant as a social and recreation center.

Compared with the cost of such facilities and their use when separated from the school plant, the economy of the combined playground, workshop, and school plant is indeed surprising. The city of Chicago has a most elaborate system of recreation parks and field-houses. Selecting the eleven most successful parks of the South Park Commission, we may compare the total cost and use of the eleven parks with the cost and use of one Gary school plant. Note that the attendance of the parks is the total, not the average, for the eleven parks. Also note that the cost of the school includes the furnishing of complete school facilities for twenty-seven hundred children, in addition to the social and recreation features.

Chicago parks and Gary school compared as to costs

Items	*Total for eleven parks in Chicago*	*One school in Gary*
Population	800,000	20,000
First cost, less land	$2,000,000	$300,000
Annual maintenance	$440,000	$100,000
Annual attendance: —		
Indoor gymnasium	310,000	1,000,000
Shower baths	1,385,000	500,000
Outdoor gymnasium	2,000,000	2,000,000
Swimming-pool	735,000	300,000
Assembly halls	270,000	1,000,000
Reading-rooms	600,000	1,000,000
Clubrooms	70,000	50,000
Lunchrooms	520,000	20,000

V

TABLE SHOWING HOW CAPACITY OF SMALL SCHOOL PLANT MAY BE DOUBLED

Increasing School Capacity

A — Traditional school plant: 8 rooms; 320 children; grounds 160 x 160; playgrounds, 80 x 160, 40 square feet per pupil: —

Cost of building and equipment	$55,000
Cost of land	5,000
10 per cent on investment	6,000
Annual operation	2,000
Cost of instruction per year	10,000

B — Gary plan for 320 more pupils: —

Additional cost of land	$5,000
Additional cost of instruction per year	10,000

Costs of building and equipment, operation and maintenance not increased, though capacity is doubled.

EPILOGUE

INTRODUCTION

Adeline and Murray Levine

BOURNE'S *The Gary Schools* is a highly positive description of a city school system that grew and developed in recognition of social need. William Wirt understood that Gary needed a modern school system, and he produced a system different in curriculum, method, and organization from the typical schools of his time. Bourne, and countless others who visited Gary, came away with the impression that Wirt was wholly successful in achieving his purposes. However, these impressions sometimes were based upon rather hurried observation.[1] Evidently there were few neutral observers of Gary. Visitors seemed ready to believe and to overlook

[1]Evelyn Dewey, for example, visited Gary as part of the research for *Schools of Tomorrow*, the book she wrote with her father, John. She planned to spend no more than three days in Gary: "... as Dutton wishes to bring out Professor Dewey's book in the fall, I have a very short time for visiting." (Letter from Evelyn Dewey to W. A. Wirt, May 14, 1914.)

flaws, or they disbelieved and came prepared to find flaws. Certainly parents who visited Gary and saw such joy in the children that they were ready to move to Gary so their children could go to school there were looking at something different than was the superintendent of schools who visited and saw nothing but unruly children and a line of crumpled papers on the floor leading directly to Wirt's own desk (Swift, 1916).

How does one decide how well a school is doing its job? Moreover, how does one go about looking at a school system different in concept and in method from the traditional school? How does one decide whether the new kind of school is attaining *its* goals? Does one measure it with old yardsticks, or are new criteria necessary? And when we are looking at a different school system, shouldn't we ask questions about how the new was implemented, and how well it was implemented? We cannot fully appreciate the outcome of a process of education without understanding the process itself. Further, if the new is the model, what problems can be anticipated if the attempt is made to transpose the new into some other setting? The change process is poorly understood, but it is predictable that attempts at change will bring about resistance and conflict (Bennis, 1966; Bennis, Benne, and Chin, 1961). Often enough, the best we can expect is that not much will change, especially in schools (Sarason, in press).

Fortunately a detailed evaluative study of the Gary school system is available, and it is addressed to the questions set down in the preceding paragraph. We will present much of that study here, for the description of the Gary schools by Bourne and the critique and evaluation by Flexner and Bachman complement each other. Bourne is the advocate of the new; he sees only the good and envisions the millennium. Flexner and Bachman are more cautious in their examination and assessment of the system.

Abraham Flexner (1866–1957) was a noted educator, best known for a report on medical education in the United States. The report, sponsored by the Carnegie Foundation for the Advancement of Teaching in 1910, is widely credited with shaping modern medical education. From 1913 to 1929 he was Assistant Secretary, Executive Secretary, and a member of the Board of the Rockefeller-funded General Education Board. That foundation endowed many small liberal arts colleges and medical schools, and it supported secondary education for Negroes. Later, Flexner helped to organize the Institute for Advanced Studies in Princeton, New Jersey; he became the first director, served in that position for nine years, and then continued on emeritus. He was considered an implacable critic of education, who launched sweeping attacks on educational institutions to help bring about reforms. In his post with the General Education Board, he had access to financial resources to support and reward institutions meeting his standards.

There are many curious points about the study of the Gary schools undertaken by Flexner for the General Education Board.[2]

[2]If one were to read Flexner's autobiography, *I Remember*, in the version published in 1940, one would get little inkling that Flexner had supported Wirt and was involved in bringing Wirt to New York. The revised version of his autobiography (1960) doesn't so much as mention the Gary story at all.

At the time the study was initiated, Flexner was a member of the Board of Education of New York City and apparently an advocate of the Garyizing of the New York schools. He solicited an invitation from Wirt[3] to undertake a scientific study of the Gary schools, ostensibly because there was so much interest that an objective and dispassionate view of the schools was necessary. At the time the study was undertaken, Flexner was already thinking of developing the small, elitist Lincoln School, at Columbia University with Rockefeller funds. The Lincoln School was to be the realization of Flexner's ideas about education expressed in his short treatise entitled *The Modern School* (Flexner, 1916).

Moreover, for whatever reason, and there

Flexner's entry in *Who Was Who* fails to list the Flexner and Bachman volume among his publications, and his front-page obituary in the *New York Times* also makes no mention of his service in public education, or his connection to the Gary schools. His reaction seems unusual and leads a psychologically minded observer to speculate about the dynamics of repression and denial.

[3]Letters from Abraham Flexner to William Wirt, June 23, 1915; July 13, 1915; letter from William Wirt to Abraham Flexner, July 8, 1915.

may have been extenuating circumstances,[4] Flexner chose Frank P. Bachman for his field director. Bachman, eminently qualified as a school administrator who had made his professional reputation writing about school organization, may have been a rather brusque, ill-spoken individual who rubbed others the wrong way (Flexner, 1940). Certainly, such characteristics were not ideal for the field director of a study of an educational institution. Bachman is said to have declared himself violently opposed to the Gary concept just a few months before the study was undertaken, and there is reason to believe that Flexner knew of Bachman's views when he commissioned him to do the study.[5]

We present these data to the reader, not because we are convinced that the Flexner and Bachman report is unreasonably biased, but because it is essential to note that research is always undertaken from some

[4]Flexner initially offered the direction of the study to Elwood Cubberly, who was interested but turned it down because he could not devote the necessary time to the study.

[5]Letter from Bessie C. Stern to William A. Wirt, March 2, 1915.

perspective, and a perspective that produces data critical of one position also supports another (Gouldner, 1968). Moreover, Flexner's choice of educational experts to conduct the study illustrates an important principle of evaluative research (Graziano, 1969). Innovations critical of established practice are referred back for evaluation to men who have made their professional reputations as creators, advocates, practitioners, or teachers of the conventional wisdom that is now either implicitly or explicitly criticized by the innovation they are evaluating. Evaluation of large-scale public enterprises can never be conducted with a scientifically neutral and dispassionate stance. Somebody will win and somebody will lose politically, socially, or financially when large-scale, public tax-supported enterprises are evaluated (Levine and Graziano, in press).

Negotiations for the General Education Board study of the Gary schools went on during the summer of 1915. The field studies began in February 1916 and continued through June 1916, although correspondence with requests for further data and clarification of the issues continued for some months afterward. The report was not published until late in 1918,[6] partly because Flexner had Wirt review the manuscripts as they were written, and Wirt, in turn, checked details with his own staff. These critical reviews of the manuscripts led to some revision of them and unquestionably added delays. Preliminary reports were not published either, although rumors concerning the content and the verdict of the Rockefeller Foundation report circulated throughout the educational world and caused Wirt professional embarrassment.[7] It is a reflection of Wirt's commitment that he took many of the criticisms seriously and acted almost at once to have his staff implement changes to improve his schools.

When the reports were actually published,

[6]There is reason to believe that the Flexner and Bachman report may have been suppressed until after the fateful New York Mayoralty election of 1917. The incumbent, John Purroy Mitchel, the Republican-Fusion candidate, had stood on his advocacy of the introduction of the Gary plan into New York City, and a Rockefeller Foundation report critical of his school plan would have been embarrassing (Cohen, 1964: *School and Society*, October 17, 1916; letter from William A. Wirt to Abraham Flexner, April 6, 1918).

[7]Letters from William Wirt to Abraham Flexner, April 6, 1918; April 16, 1918; from Abraham Flexner to William Wirt, April 9, 1918.

a year had passed since the October 1917 school riots against the Gary plan and the election victory of anti-Gary city officials. Furthermore, public concern was focused on our entry into the First World War, and interest diminished in the Gary plan. *The Reader's Guide to Periodic Literature* lists seventy-six items about the Gary schools from 1915 to 1918, and then but four items in the next four years. Interest in the Gary plan revived in the 1920s; there was a strong demand for school building in the postwar period, and the duplicate school feature promised important economies (Callahan, 1962).[8]

[8]Flexner's 1940 claim that his report effectively killed public interest in the Gary plan is a patent overstatement. One might interpret his statement to mean that the report killed interest in the Gary plan among the wealthy who contribute money to foundations that support educational practices. One can raise some rather interesting issues concerning the ways in which foundations use evaluative research. Do they use such research to inform the public generally, or is much of what they do for "in-house" purposes, and designed to inform only the foundations policy makers? The Ford Foundation, for example, recently denied us access to its report on Oakland, California, cited in Marris and Rein (1967) on the grounds that it was for internal use only. Marris and Rein, with financial support from Ford, wrote an evaluative report of Ford-funded programs. How does such a failure to make research information publically available square with their tax-exempt status and their sponsorship of work that vitally influences public institutions?

The Gary Schools: A General Account is the summary volume of the General Education Board's study of the Gary schools. The entire report is presented in seven additional volumes. The chapters of the summary volume consolidate the results reported in the previous seven volumes and include a description of Gary, its population, its school plants, and the duplicate plan. In this section we present an abridged version of the summary volume. We have attempted to retain some of the detail and the summary statements to give the reader an idea of how the Rockefeller experts viewed the Gary system. Chapter IV on Administration and Supervision, Chapter VII on Classroom Instruction, and Chapter XVI, Conclusion, are included in full. The problems discussed in these chapters are probably as important today in school innovation as they were in that day. The New York City More Effective Schools program foundercd precisely because supervision was a problem, the reeducation of teachers was a problem, and serious attention to the problem of evaluation and change was lacking (Levine and Graziano, in press). The remaining chapters have been abridged heavily or entirely omitted. We have retained pages or paragraphs that give a feeling for the nature of the problems noted and have interspersed commentary, in the form of footnotes,[9] to point up some significant issues in the evaluative study. We have tried neither to distort the criticism by our selections nor to exhibit great biases in pointing out unrecognized value assumptions in the critical reports. The Flexner and Bachman presentation of Gary is in many respects accurate, but their view of Gary raises the critical question of how one measures and what one values in schools. At what cost in enjoyment do we gain measurable advantage on achievement tests? Should the achievement test criterion be permitted to have such absolute dominance in the schools? How can we evaluate the life-giving potential of the schools in which our children and their teachers spend their days?

[9]Our footnotes are numbered consecutively in each of the following chapters. The original footnotes are indicated by an asterisk.

THE GARY SCHOOLS:

A General Account
by
Abraham Flexner
and
Frank P. Bachman

Abridged and annotated by
Adeline and Murray Levine

[Chapters I, II, and III are a description of Gary, its history, its population, the school plant, and the general organization of the schools. Much of the material overlaps that provided by Bourne.]

IV

ADMINISTRATION AND SUPERVISION*

THE MANAGEMENT of a system of schools conducted on the Gary plan is obviously a highly complicated affair. Despite the fact that the success of such a system depends very largely on effective management, it is not easy to tell precisely what the administrative and supervisory arrangements of the Gary schools are. At the head stands the superintendent. The superintendent of schools in an American city has usually both business and educational duties; directly as well as through assistants he carries out the provisions of the law and the orders of the board of education in respect to all matters involving business, and, in the same way, both directly and through assistants, exercises general control of educational policies — meeting supervisors and the teaching staff for conference, calling for examinations and

*For detailed account, see report on Organization and Administration, by George D. Strayer and Frank P. Bachman. [New York: General Education Board, 1918 (Eds.)]

reports, and, as occasion offers, visiting classrooms and laboratories, now for the purpose of making an inspection, again to satisfy himself as to the quality of some special classroom procedure, or the competency of particular individuals.[1] The activities in progress are so many, even in a small system, that no superintendent can possibly keep in constant touch with all; but there is assuredly danger of collapse somewhere unless the superintendent's hand is distinctly felt in both the main fields of his responsibility—business management and education.

In consequence of the repeated and prolonged absences[2] of the superintendent during

[1]Having read through a dozen years of Wirt's correspondence, we are convinced that the job of Superintendent is highly complex and varied. To float a bond issue, settle an irate parent, decide on toilet paper, address a governmental body, hire teachers and mediate disputes all on the same day is indeed taxing. (Eds.)

[2]Among the hazards of success are the demands of people who visit the successful project, and the demands made on the innovators to consult and lecture elsewhere. If the initial success of a project depended on the loving care and attention to detail lavished on it by its originators, a project can truly suffer when other demands are made on its staff. We feel that few projects take this hazard to heart, although every successful venture runs into it. How much the deficiencies Flexner and Bachman observed are attributable to some such factor is indeterminate. (Eds.)

the year 1915–16, central control at Gary appeared to be limited to general direction, mostly on the business side. Educational supervision was of a general character only. The superintendent gave time and thought to plans connected with building and similar needs, selected and assigned teachers, received written and oral reports from the assistant superintendents and school principals, and explained the broad educational aims and policies to the staff. The execution of educational details did not, however, come directly within his sphere. In other words, of the two important concerns of the ordinary city superintendent, the supervisory function did not seem to bulk large.

Supervision fell almost altogether to assistants — an assistant superintendent who directs the night schools and supervises the higher elementary grades, an assistant superintendent in charge of kindergarten and primary grades, a supervisor or special teacher of handwriting, a supervisor of physical education, who also has teaching duties, a supervisor of the industrial arts, who at the same time has charge of repairs, certain heads of high school departments, who, though teachers, appear to have a sort of general responsibility for their several subjects throughout the system, and school principals.

The theory of general supervision, which accords with the practice observed, can best be expressed by saying that the assistant superintendents, and all supervisors, for that matter, develop plans and outline ideals in accordance with the Gary plan, and then leave the teaching staff largely to realize these aims in their own way. However, it is not to be inferred from this that the assistant superintendents are not concerned with the efficiency of the schools. They hold teachers' meetings three or four times a year; they visit classes, inspecting the instruction and making suggestions for its improvement, and finally grade the teachers. They give a good deal of attention to the needs of individual pupils, seeing that they are properly classified; to this end, they assemble reports on children's work, determine whether or not they shall be promoted, and oversee the make-up of their daily programs and the organization of classes.

The special supervisors deal with given branches of instruction only—the handwriting supervisor, for example, with handwriting. This particular special supervisor corresponds, however, more nearly to what is known as a special teacher. He goes from building to building and room to room actually teaching classes, particularly of the upper grades; at the same time, he counsels teachers, gives suggestions about their work, and at long intervals brings them together for conference. The supervisor of physical training works in much the same way.

The supervisor of the industrial and household arts, as stated before, also looks after repairs for the entire system, and oversees some of the new constructive work. He is in and out of the several shops and even the cooking and sewing rooms almost daily and knows in a general way what is going on in every shop. He also meets with the shopmen two or three times a year for an evening's discussion of their problems.

The school principal is an executive or administrative, rather than a supervisory, officer. He has, indeed, little to do with the educational side of the school. After organizing his school in consultation with the superintendent and assistant superintendents, he looks after the building and grounds, meets parents, handles special attendance and discipline cases, orders books and supplies, and makes reports to the superintendent; he also arranges the programs of teachers and supplies substitutes, holds weekly teachers' meetings after school hours, and occasionally visits classes; but he has no responsibility for the quality of the teaching. Records of enrollment, of promotion, and of scholarship come to his office, but the responsibility for what pupils do and for their promotion belongs to the teachers and general supervisors.

These supervisory arrangements are hardly calculated to meet the unusual problems that arise in a situation as complicated and novel as that at Gary.[3] Supervision of the

[3]Is there an implication that a more traditional supervisory arrangement would have been more effective? Certainly the educational administrators do not question the point, although traditional supervision was under fire publically (e.g., *New York Times*, December 2, 1917). Is this an example of Graziano's (1969) principle that innovations critical of a power structure are referred back to that power structure for evaluation? (Eds.)

kind described is not likely to determine whether departures from conventional practice do or do not make good, nor is it likely to overcome the obstacles arising from the quality and antecedents of the pupils. In the course of these pages, these statements will be more than once justified. But it is worth while in this connection to record a few instances of administrative and supervisory laxity, such as tend to obscure or defeat the demonstration of some of Gary's innovations.

We have referred to the fact that young children are regularly detailed to act as "helpers" or "observers" to older pupils engaged in shop or laboratory work, while older pupils frequently take charge of classes, assist in keeping records, correct papers, etc. This practice is defended on the ground that participation in such responsibilities is educative, since it reproduces an important human relationship. But does it work? As we shall see in subsequent chapters, our own investigations suggest, in the main, a negative answer. Would it work if efficiently controlled? That, of course, no one can yet say. A striking though not essential characteristic of the Gary system is thus imperiled because its operation has not been carefully watched.

Again, we have called attention to the unusual sequence of studies sometimes followed. We have pointed out that class schedules are so arranged that one class will play in the early morning and do its work in the early afternoon, while another class — or the same class another term — reverses the arrangement. Now, is there any reason why children should not play in the early hours of the morning and do their classroom work in the early hours of the afternoon? Gary assumes and believes that there is no objection. Is there? No one really knows. The question lends itself, however, to experimental inquiry. Given classes might readily be carried for a series of years alternating the former arrangement with the latter, while others are carried with the common order of studies. A series of graphs might show whether the level of class work is affected by the factor here under discussion. Or, perhaps some other experiment could be devised for the purpose of determining the question. Similar questions should be asked in reference to the wisdom of extending departmentalization into the lowest grades. In any event, these are experimental problems to be worked out coöperatively by the teachers and supervising staff; but supervision in this sense — the very type required by a system rich in novelties and possibilities — has not been instituted.

One more illustration may be employed. Diversity of facilities and activities coupled with the unusual length of the school day makes for flexibility of program. Gary indeed believes that its program is more nicely adjusted to the individual child than is the case elsewhere. To what extent and in what sense is this true? The term "flexible" is properly applied to leeway used in order to defer to a particular child's need or opportunity. A child may be backward or unusually capable; a "flexible" curriculum places him accordingly. Flexibility has nothing to do with accident, caprice, or instability, all of which are hostile to the formation of good habit. The Gary organization lends itself to individual adjustments, but whether or not they are wisely made depends on administrative supervision. Thus, for instance, a seventh grade class (No. 44) in the Froebel school contained many weak pupils in unquestionable need of individual consideration and attention. Its official spring program was as follows:

8:15	Gymnasium (play) or library
9:15	Music
10:15	Arithmetic
11:15	English
12:15	Luncheon
1:15	Auditorium
2:15	Shop (boys); Cooking or sewing (girls)
3:15	United States history

The entire class of 31 pupils recited together in arithmetic at the scheduled time. Only two other subjects, gymnasium and English, were pursued by all members, but in neither of these branches were they all in the same class. Twenty three took no music, seven no history, and four did not attend the auditorium. On the surface, these variations might be interpreted as representing real educational adjustments. In point of fact, they were not adjustments to serve the interests of particular pupils or to secure their regular advancement, but merely chance arrangements, the product of loose administration and supervision.

The most surprising variations occur in the 9:15 and 2:15 periods. At 9:15 the class is scheduled for music. At that time, thirteen pupils were in the gymnasium, seven were taking music, one arithmetic, two shop, six cooking or sewing, and two drawing. At 2:15 the boys were supposed to be in shop and girls in cooking or sewing. Actually, eight went to gymnasium or library, one to music, seven to shop, nine to cooking or sewing, five to drawing, and one to history. Again, the official program calls for only one period a day in each of the several studies; and yet fourteen pupils took two hours of gymnasium or library and two took three hours. Twelve pupils did double and one treble duty in practical work. All told, there were thus not less than fifty four deviations from the official class program, but only three were to afford additional academic instruction — one in arithmetic and two in English. All persons concerned — teachers, principal, and children — were questioned about these changes. The principal, whose written endorsement is required, had no recollection of the reasons for them and no record of them. Although the pupil's Program Card reads, "No dropping of class nor change of program will be permitted without the written consent of the assistant superintendent," the children had not consulted that official. A teacher employed to advise with children about their practical work could throw no light on the situation. Register teachers,* supposed to have on file "Permission to Change Class" slips, had barely a half dozen of them — not one completely executed — and were, therefore, almost wholly unaware of what had happened. The truth is that, in a few instances, the regular teachers, on their own authority, had excused pupils from their classes, but in most instances children had dropped what they did not want and elected what they wanted, provided they could get it, without consulting anybody. Prolonged inquiry showed clearly that with five or six

*Seventeen register teachers kept the records of this one class, each doing a part of the work.

exceptions all the changes were the result of childish caprice exercised without restraint.[4]

Nor does class 44 stand alone. Out of eleven additional Froebel and Emerson classes similarly tabulated, in six there was not a single pupil taking double work in any of the regular studies, and in the remaining five, not more than a single pupil in any one of them. In no class were there as many deviations from the official program in special work as in class 44. Still, such deviations as there were, were rarely educational adjustments; they were due mostly to the child's own choice, or to accidents of organization at the time.

The upshot of our consideration of the Gary plan and the Gary organization may be put into a few words. The Gary plan is as

[4]We do not mean to condone mindless permissiveness. However, we question whether the authors understood or appreciated the problems of schools in poorer areas. Was this really a matter of childish caprice, or was it related to the atmosphere of the Froebel school, which served the poorer part of town. Would the school's atmosphere have been the same if these working-class and immigrant children were held to a rigid schedule? Moreover, Bourne (pp. 109–110) views exactly the same phenomenon as a matter of planning on the part of school administrators, an attempt to satisfy curiosity and to provide freer, more rational choices. (Eds.)

large and intelligent a conception as has yet been reached in respect to the scope and bearing of public education. The administrative scheme by which Gary undertakes to carry out the plan is ingenious to the point of originality. The arrangements for controlling and supervising the operation of the scheme are, however, defective; there is, therefore, reason to fear that the execution of the plan will fall short of the conception.

[Chapters V and VI provide a detailed description of the course of study (e.g., hours devoted to various subjects) and statistical data concerning the teaching staff.]

VII

CLASSROOM INSTRUCTION*

WE HAVE now discussed the main factors that determine the content and quality of classroom instruction — organization, supervision, course of study, teaching staff. We learned that the course of study is, in the first instance, necessarily that outlined by the state; that the members of the teaching staff do not differ essentially in education, training, and experience from the corresponding types of teacher in other systems; finally, that, while the Gary system is devoted to a modern conception of education, supervision has

*This chapter deals with the teaching of reading, composition, spelling, arithmetic, geography, and history in the elementary schools, and with English, French, German, mathematics, Latin, and history in the high schools; science, shop work, etc., are dealt with in special chapters and special reports.

A tabular statement showing the amount of observation of classes on which the present chapter is based is given in Appendix A, page 210.

[One hundred teachers were observed for 176 hours over 228 lessons. Forty-five teachers were observed once; thirty-five, twice; and twenty, three or four times. (Eds.)]

been too uncertain to mold the teaching staff into an effective organ for concerted effort toward its achievement.

A moment's consideration will, however, show that under even the most favorable conditions an entire school system can only gradually promote radical reform in the substance and manner of classroom instruction. The course of study may indeed be expressed in terms so general that large leeway is left to the grade teacher; principal and supervisors may be favorable to innovation; the fact remains that at this day the conventional training of the teachers and the conventional character of available textbooks in most subjects, generally speaking, handicap wide departure by an entire system from established practices.[1]

In the case of Gary, certain special factors already mentioned should also be taken into account. The population being foreign, the children come in large numbers from homes

[1]It is highly characteristic of teachers to claim that they are not permitted or encouraged to be innovative; administrators claim that teachers resist innovation, and insist on having defined curricula and approved methods (Sarason, in press). (Eds.)

where no English or very poor English is spoken; the increase in population is taking place so rapidly that there is a steady infiltration into the schools of new and crude, even though ultimately promising, material; finally, the teaching staff, expanded to meet the pressure described, is composed of teachers of such varied training and experience that unity of purpose is extremely difficult to obtain.

One gathers the impression that, carried along by its splendid conception of public education but misled, perhaps, by the ease with which an adequate material embodiment was so swiftly attained in the Froebel and Emerson plants,[2] Gary failed to appreciate the extreme difficulty of converting new educational principles into new educational practice. It would be both unjust and unwise to make too much of this error, for it does not disprove the fundamental soundness of the

[2]It is true to this day that brick-and-mortar innovation is much easier than program innovation, and that the two are frequently confused. The development of Community Mental Health Centers, which do more of the same, offering "old wine in new bottles," is a case in point in a field other than education. (Eds.)

scheme or destroy its stimulating influence on public education. The truth is that anything like general success was at the outset impossible, because of the lack of proper tools and proper agents. Had this been clearly perceived, doubtless details would have been more carefully watched and thus a larger measure of practical success would undoubtedly have been attained. In the present and succeeding chapters the actual teaching at Gary will be described in the effort to present an objective account of the instruction offered, as respects both content and quality. In view of the fact, however, that serious defects will be pointed out, the authors drop this word of caution lest the real scope, courage, and intelligence of the Gary vision be obscured by the errors made in the first attempts toward its realization.

We have said that thoroughgoing reform can proceed only as a new body of teaching material is developed and teachers of a new type are trained. Fortunately, the situation has in recent years been ameliorated by the diffusion among teachers of sounder ideas as to values and methods and by the publication of a large body of supplementary school texts in the principal classroom subjects. Even teachers trained in the most cut and dried fashion have in large numbers been aroused to the futility of abstract drill in grammar and arithmetic and to the uselessness of a mechanical grind in geography and history; and though the textbooks in common use continue to contain much irrelevant, uninteresting, and indigestible detail, the intelligent and resourceful teacher is not usually so strictly and unsympathetically "supervised" that she is kept from supplementing or partly supplanting the textbook by utilizing materials and paraphernalia rich in content and in emotional value. While, as we have said, it would be unfair at this stage to expect any school system to organize its classroom instruction on a consistently modern basis, it is entirely fair to demand that the formal methods and sterile material of a past generation should be noticeably relieved by the introduction of a fresher spirit and by the use of concrete and fertile subject matter.

In so far as classroom instruction is concerned, the Gary schools show the confusion inevitably incident to transition, but aggravated unquestionably by ineffectiveness of central control. The conventional school framework has been shattered; new ends, new activities have been freely introduced; directly and indirectly, the inadequacy or unsoundness of certain common school aims has been emphasized. Self-control, initiative, resourcefulness have been very properly set up as essential characteristics of training for life in a democratic society. Unfortunately, many of the teachers have not been at Gary long enough to catch the spirit; some who sympathize with its spirit have not been effectively assisted to abandon or modify their former habits; in consequence, despite some excellent work, which we do not overlook, many teachers at Gary are probably not doing so well as they have previously done under other conditions.[3]

[3]There is an implication that the traditional supervisory structure was a necessary aspect of school organization. Teachers are viewed as people who cannot function without direction by supervisors. Flexner had earlier expressed such a view of New York City teachers when he was a member of the New York City Board of Education (*New York Times*, May 28, 1914). Such a view of teachers by administrators seems to be an integral aspect of school culture, even today (Sarason, in press). (Eds.)

These statements are particularly true of the regular primary teachers. They devote two hours daily to work in the three R's, but departmentalization tends in a measure to interfere with the direct use of literature, science, and games as means of making the three R's less formal and more appealing. The danger — never far distant — that the work of the primary teacher will be technical and mechanical is therefore increased at Gary. A teacher might, of course, even under this organization, so familiarize herself with what her pupils are doing in the special branches that she would be able to bring what they have learned in them to bear upon the mastery of the regular studies. Most of those observed were not doing so. Primary instruction too rarely radiated from a central topic, from which were derived the materials for reading, spelling, language, arithmetic, handwork, dramatization, and even science and music, each portion thus reënforcing every other part; it was more apt to be handled in separate compartments, arithmetic, language, reading being more or less independent of one another, with the result that much of the primary teaching was mechanical and slow. This was not, be it repeated, universally the case; but it was the rule, rather than the exception.

Take reading for an example. Some excellent instruction in beginning classes was observed. Appropriate stories about familiar objects were developed by the teachers and written on the blackboard for the children to read; phrase reading and natural expression received attention; the meaning of the new words selected for mastery was conveyed through the use of the children's experiences, real objects, picture cards, and action; and well directed repetition through the use of the blackboard and picture word cards pressed home the desired word image. Such teaching represents the occasional "high points." More commonly appropriate preparatory work was slighted; inadequate emphasis was given to the meaning of new words and to the development of a well chosen reading vocabulary; the children imitated the standard of expression set by the teacher and under such conditions the reading became mere word naming.

Of the reading heard in the upper primary grades, some of it was good, but in the main it ranged from ordinary to poor. The selections were usually excellent, comprising the best of myths, fairy tales, fables, folklore, poems, and descriptive narrations of famous events and characters — that is, the best available material had been selected, but the teaching technique was often seriously at fault. The pupils of a room were, as a rule, divided into two sections, one reciting, while the other did seat or board work. The section engaged in reading occupied kindergarten chairs about the teacher. The children had seldom made any preparation; seldom did the teacher ask the subject of the lesson or seek to bring out the main theme. She merely directed the children to prepare silently the first sentence or paragraph. On the completion of this task, the pupils raised their hands; thereupon a pupil began. The teacher might ask a question to introduce the next story or paragraph, but more frequently she called upon a child to read on; and thereafter the exercises became sight work. If pronunciation became too bad, the teacher might write the words upon the blackboard for drill. Little attention was devoted to meaning or use. Only once in the classes observed were children required to re-tell the story or to summarize the main points of the narration after the reading. Classes were usually dismissed without assignments, and even when assignments were made the teacher did not regularly give suggestions as to the preparation of the new lesson. The work was too frequently characterized by listlessness and indifference; after the first few minutes of the period only part of the class appeared to attend to the work in hand.[4]

After reading, the time remaining to the regular primary teachers is taken up mostly with spelling, writing, and arithmetic. In spelling, common words chosen by the teacher

[4]The effect of the observer is not considered. While Gary teachers and children should have been accustomed to classroom observers, a few of the teachers complained to Wirt they felt intimidated by the Rockefeller experts who let it be known they considered themselves the ultimate authorities on education. Some said the observers actively interfered in their classrooms and made openly hostile or disparaging remarks to them. It is not clear how widely shared this experience was among Gary teachers, but if it happened a few times early in the study, the school's grapevine would have passed it on immediately, and others would have felt intimidated, even in the absence of overt acts by the observers. (Eds.)

from the daily life of the children and from their current school work were emphasized, and well selected lists were also supplied by the primary supervisor. Patience was exhibited in drilling children in the number combinations and in the fundamental processes. No small part of the drill in these subjects was carried on by helpers — children from the sixth, seventh, and eighth grades. By way of creating interest in drill, competitive devices were freely employed. For example, a competitive game was thus made of spelling: The teacher wrote the words on the blackboard — "snow," "cow," "foreign," etc. After the children had studied these for a moment, the teacher called by turns, from the two sides into which the class had been divided, upon the children, who indicated by raising the hand that they were ready. The pupil signaled took his place before the class, with his back to the blackboard, and endeavored to pronounce and spell each of the words of the lists. The side which had the greater number of successes to its credit won the contest. The difficulty with these competitive devices is that the same aggressive children were always in evidence, while the timid and the children who are probably in greatest need of individual attention kept to their seats. Little was done toward using the more recently contrived methods for the teaching of primary spelling or primary arithmetic.

In the middle and upper grades some efforts to vitalize arithmetic were observed. To make the topic of stocks and bonds real, an upper grade teacher organized his class into a joint stock company for the time being. There is also displayed in the hall of Emerson some work showing the application of percentage to baseball club standings, and a graph of the temperature of a schoolroom at different hours of the day. But for the most part, in these grades, the best teaching of arithmetic seen was of the old-fashioned sort, where children are held rigorously to a mastery of processes and to the solution and explanation of problems of every conceivable kind.[5] Few signs of the new arithmetic were

[5]There is no evidence in the achievement test data (see Ch. VIII) that Gary children did comparatively better in arithmetic than in other subjects. (Eds.)

noted. For example, two middle grade classes were learning liquid measure. In the one, the teacher exhibited a gill, a pint, a quart, a half gallon, and a gallon measure. But there was nothing for the children to measure; they merely looked at the measures, observing their relative sizes. In the second class, the table of liquid measures was presented altogether as something to be memorized from the book. There were no measures for the children to handle and compare, nothing to measure, no appeal to experience, no mention of use.[6]

In the higher grades a few teachers were doing well in reading. The selections, generally of excellent character, were studied seriously. Interpretive discussion preceded oral reading. Appreciation and taste were conscious objects of the instruction, and the selections were employed to present in concrete form the larger ideals of successful personal and community living. But the bulk of the reading in both the middle and upper grades was not of high quality. As in the

[6]See Sarason (in press) for a description of similar problems in the introduction of new math after Sputnik. (Eds.)

primary grades, the pupils were too often listless and indifferent.

Periods devoted to history and geography were usually divided equally between so-called study — a form of silent reading — and recitation. There was no supervised study. Lessons were invariably assigned by pages or by general subject, mostly without comment by the teacher. The children read over the assignments chiefly with a view to finding the answers to the questions printed at the end of the section. At the end of the allotted study period, the recitation began. The teacher, with book in hand, put seriatim the above mentioned questions, occasionally adding one or more on her own initiative. For example, if in history: "What was Jefferson's purpose in securing the passage of the Embargo Act?" "What was the Embargo Act?" etc. Or in geography: "In what part of the United States is New England?" "Name the states." "Which state is largest?" etc. The answers of the children were brief and deficient in detail; this, whether they remembered for the moment what the text contained or whether they read the answers from the open books before them. The teacher usually added very little; there was little or no class discussion, outside reading was seldom required. Some of the seventh and eighth grade geography and history, and almost all that of the middle grades, was indeed little more than a sight reading exercise.

As in the primary grades there was usually in the middle and upper grades too little connection between the different parts of a pupil's daily work. In part, this is due to the fact that in the higher grades the "fundamentals" are sometimes distributed among several teachers. Making clear to children the cross relations existing between studies is nowhere easy, and departmentalization rather increases the difficulty at Gary. But more could be accomplished than is now attempted. The teaching of arithmetic, for example, could take more account of what is going on in the laboratories, the shops, the cooking and sewing rooms; the influence of geography upon history could be more frequently pointed out. The main evidences of correlation noted were the effort to bring into the spelling lesson words common to the special and practical activities; and a similar and sometimes remarkably successful effort to draw composition themes from the shops, the laboratories, and the gymnasium or playground. A really admirable paper on swimming, in which abundant material was systematically organized and clearly presented, is a case in point.

The generally meager and formal character of the classroom instruction may be in part due to the assumption that exercises in shops and laboratories, reading in connection with science, history, and industry will supply the vital elements which mere drill omits. To what extent this is the case will appear in the chapters dealing with the activities in question, and in the chapter describing the objective tests designed to measure skill in reading, spelling, arithmetic, and composition.

In a measure, excessive formality in regular classroom work may arise from the theory that an application teacher is provided, whose special concern it is to assist backward pupils and to place "before the children real problems of the type that the world of industry, business, and citizenship will place before them when they leave school." Without raising any question as to the wisdom of divorcing the child's learning of fundamental processes from the application of those processes, the facts at Gary do not bear out the theory of a separate application teacher. There were only four application teachers in the system during the spring term 1916, of whom one gave regular departmental instruction, while the remaining three confined their efforts to the lower middle and primary grades. Observation of the work revealed nothing beyond the same kind of formal drill upon elements and processes that was observed in regular classes. Moreover, application teachers are handicapped by not knowing intimately the precise ground covered by the class teacher and the particular difficulties of the children in hand.[7] The same amount of

[7]We do not know why the attempt at coordinated teaching did so poorly. We believe the problem may have been caused, in part, by interpersonal difficulties between supervisors. Wirt's correspondence and papers contain memos indicating jealousies and internecine warfare among some of his supervisory personnel. Then as now, cooperation may have been legislated as a moral obligation, ignoring human foibles. Should planners *routinely* take the contingencies of social interaction into account? (Eds.)

time could certainly be employed to better advantage in regular work of proper type.

It is not easy to make out how classroom instruction as a whole is affected by departmentalization. In the earlier grades excessive departmentalization may tend to separate into independent teaching units subjects which at that stage might better be presented by one teacher, constantly solicitous to connect activities one with another. On the other hand, it is doubtful whether in the middle and upper grades departmentalization is complete enough to procure real continuity in the teaching of the regular classroom studies. For in these grades pupils change teachers in the fundamental subjects on advancing from the third to the fourth grade, and also on passing from the sixth to the seventh. Unquestionably, the Gary type of program requires more departmental teaching than the conventional school, but efficient supervision and careful organization can alone secure for the pupil the advantages inherent in it.

Of the high school subjects, no departure from conventional handling was observed in mathematics. In the Emerson school the teacher of Latin had undertaken to relate the instruction in Latin to English and to everyday life and her efforts unquestionably aroused enthusiastic interest on the part of her pupils. In both schools, the spoken use of French and German was stressed; and general history was taught with conscious reference to the requirements of citizenship. But much the most important novelty was the work in English composition, already alluded to above.

Instead of short daily or weekly themes, an entire term was concentrated upon a single effort. The work was done not hurriedly at home, but deliberately at school. All the steps necessary to successful writing were taken in consultation with and under the direction of the teacher. A practical atmosphere surrounded the work, and it was executed as nearly as possible in the spirit of the professional writer. Free choice of topics was permitted, but these were carefully canvassed in order to decide whether they were of sufficient general interest, timely, and worth while. Pupils were taught how to assemble data, how to observe, how to use reference books and the library, and how to take, keep, and arrange notes. With the preliminaries out of the way, the original outline was revised for the writing. The first draft was freely made, without too much regard to choice of words, form, or organization. The teacher reviewed this draft with the pupil, leading him to discover for himself its weak places and discussing with him ways to improve them, leaving him to make the needed revisions. This procedure was repeated again and again. The outcome was an elaborate essay into which the pupil had put himself and from the doing of which he had derived real training.

High school teaching was unfavorably affected by the practice of placing in one class pupils of different high school grades — a necessary expedient in the small high school. The tendency was marked in the special studies and activities; somewhat less so in the old line high school disciplines. Commercial classes almost always comprised pupils from each of the four high school years, special students of uncertain preparation, and even eighth grade children. To add to instructional difficulties, this promiscuous group usually pursued typewriting, stenography, and bookkeeping, all at the same time, under a single teacher. Mathematics classes were frequently made up of pupils from three different high school years; at times all took the same kind and grade of instruction; again each group had different work — for example, arithmetic and solid geometry, first and second term algebra. The same mixture of pupils from the different high school years occurred in Latin, modern languages, English and history. These promiscuous groupings and combinations are accounted for on the grounds of irregularity and economy.

The situation at Gary as regards instruction is thus confused. The newness of the city and of the enterprise and the ambitious scale on which the schools are projected not only account for some of the defects pointed out, but ought in fairness to be regarded as in some measure extenuating them. It is, nevertheless, clear that, so far as the modern school involves the elimination of obsolete material and the vital handling of all material in the usual classroom subjects, Gary's contribution is not considerable. The modern attitude is indeed encountered here and there in almost every subject, but, while heartily encouraged, it is still exceptional and individual rather than characteristic and general. Under existing conditions the absence of efficient supervision cuts both ways. Teachers with ideas — such as the teacher of English whose work is described above — are not hampered by a supervisor who has different notions; on the other hand, less competent instructors working amidst difficult conditions are also left to their own devices. In the main, therefore, the teaching is of ordinary type, ineffectually controlled. There is nothing in the Gary plan that requires this; there is no reason why a school of the Gary type should not be well organized, well administered, and well supervised. Indeed, as we have already urged, the enrichment of school life inevitably results in complications which give added importance to good organization, good administration, and good supervision.[8]

[8]Once again, note the unquestioned assumption that what is "good" for the new is that which was "good" for the old. The experts in administration know and do not have to think about the administrative, supervisory, and organizational structure that would promote the new goals of the school. Among those who have addressed this problem of the organization of human services, a highly sophisticated view is presented by Goldenberg (1970) for residential treatment centers. (Eds.)

VIII

CLASSROOM TESTS*

[THIS CHAPTER begins with a discussion of the need for objective measurement and the use of objective tests of school achievement, then very new instruments. The first tests discussed are of handwriting.]

A comparison of the results obtained in successive grades shows that pupils learn to write faster without learning to write much better as they go forward through the grades. . . . Comparison with the results of similar tests in other cities must, of course, be made with caution, since the methods employed are so new and the factors to be controlled so many that different situations are not strictly comparable. With this qualification, it is perhaps still worth noting that, on the whole, when compared with those of other cities,

*For detailed account, see report on Measurement of Classroom Products, by Stuart A. Courtis. [New York: General Education Board, 1919 (Eds.)]

Gary results in the free choice writing test are lower in quality. . . . Apparently, the Gary children write more freely than other children, but pay less attention to the quality of their work. On these points the three different tests practically agree. . . . And no clear difference is to be made out as between the quality of the handwriting in the various schools at Gary, that is, there is no certain evidence that one school does better or worse than another.

[The next subject to be considered is spelling. Spelling ability is judged by several different methods.]

. . . It would appear, therefore, that, as thus tested, grade by grade, the Gary children spell less well than the children of the 84 cities on which the standard of 76 per cent. used above was based; on the other hand those who remain through the twelfth grade, reach and slightly excel the common eighth grade standard. . . .

As a check upon the formal spelling tests, misspellings in papers written in the composition test were tabulated. . . . The general accuracy of the spelling was . . . very high — 97 or 98 per cent., according as slips are counted or not — a result that conflicts with that of the two tests already described. Even if the fifty common words, used altogether 14,598 times, are omitted, the percentage of the remainder correctly spelled is still high (96 per cent.). The list thus abbreviated still contains many short and easy words, but it also contains some of the so-called "spelling demons" — words commonly misspelled by children everywhere and in all grades. Hence the meaning of the discrepancy between the list tests and the composition tests must remain a matter of speculation.

[The main reasons for limiting the measurement of arithmetic achievement to the basic skills were discussed.]

The skills selected for measurement were addition, subtraction, multiplication, and division of whole numbers and fractions. These abilities are at least fundamental for all arithmetical work, both in school and in later life.

Measurement of the skill of the Gary children in carrying out the four fundamental operations with the Courtis Tests, Series B, shows regular though small gains in both rate of work and in accuracy throughout the elementary grades, a growth that continues also through the high school, except in multiplication, in which little gain in accuracy is made beyond the eighth grade. . . . In general, the Gary results compare unfavorably with scores elsewhere obtained. Thus, the Gary eighth grade children attempt 8.4 problems in addition as against 11.6 examples, the standard for small cities, and attain an accuracy of 57 per cent. as against the standard, 76 per cent. . . .

[English composition was the next subject to be evaluated. The tests and the underlying concepts were described.]

The Kansas Silent Reading tests, among others, were used to measure the silent reading of the Gary children. These consist of short paragraphs, each requiring the child to make some response; the accuracy with which the response is made indicates whether the paragraph has been correctly read and comprehended. The test is therefore not only a reading but an intelligence test, affording an index of the degree of development attained in the ability "to read and think about what is read." The results show that Gary children respond to a complicated test of this kind about as well as children generally. . . .

The results of the two chapters dealing with instruction may be briefly summarized. The impressions gained through inspection and the results of the tests are not entirely consistent. For example, silent reading makes a distinctly better showing in the tests than one would have expected on the basis of classroom observation. Spelling makes a poor showing on the list test and a very good showing on the composition test. It is not possible to reconcile these divergencies without adducing considerations as to which different opinions could fairly be entertained. Without, however, seeking to ignore the conflict of evidence, the authors still feel that the quality of classroom instruction at Gary falls short of what is necessary. . . .[1]

The Froebel and Emerson schools are the only schools completely equipped on the Gary plan; the Jefferson and Beveridge schools, though organized on the duplicate basis, offer a much simpler program. Again, the Froebel school, containing 36 per cent. of the entire school population, is more recent in origin and more foreign in composition than the Emerson. Do the results of the tests reflect these differences? Is the classroom work of the fully developed Gary schools consistently different in quality from that of the less complicated Gary schools? The facts are these:

In the handwriting tests there is almost no trace of constant differences from school to school; the differences in spelling are slight, but, such as they are, lean in favor of the Jefferson and Beveridge schools; in arithmetic, Beveridge leads, Jefferson comes

[1]Note the assertion of an evaluative statement, despite conflicting evidence. The authors make no attempt to reconcile the conflict. Moreover, even if the children do less well on the tests, what is the practical significance of the obtained differences in test scores? How much of the free atmosphere would have to be sacrificed to produce good test scores, and would it be worth it? (Eds.)

second, Froebel, despite its handicaps, surpasses Emerson; in composition, the order runs, Jefferson, Emerson, Froebel, Beveridge; in oral reading, Emerson is distinctly better than the other three schools; in silent reading Froebel and Beveridge read more rapidly than Jefferson and Emerson, while in the reproduction test, Jefferson comes first, Emerson second, and Beveridge last . . . .[2]

We are inclined to believe that lowness of score is attributable to lack of unity of effort on the part of an ineffectively supervised teaching staff, recruited from many different sources, and to confusion due to the constant infiltration of pupils from other school systems, while the fluctuations from school to school and from subject to subject are probably to be ascribed to local and individual causes. However this may be, it must be recognized that no educational system can be considered to have completely

[2]These differences are striking. They suggest to us that children of American-born parents do better in oral presentation, and the lower-class, immigrant population does better in silent work. Did the Gary system bring the lower-class group to parity with the middle-class group in some areas of study? If so, we would rate the achievement as considerable. (Eds.)

established itself until, whatever else it achieves, it has also secured the fundamental educational values represented by the essential tools of learning. The results of testing the Gary schools do not invalidate the effort to socialize education, but it is evident that the Gary experiment has not yet successfully solved the problems involved in the socialization of education, in so far as efficient instruction in the necessary common school branches is concerned.[3]

[3]The summary clearly shows the heavy weight placed on attainment on tests in the "necessary common school branches" without any indication of the human, emotional cost in teaching in ways that result in good scores on achievement tests. The specialist in educational measurement does take the efficiency of instruction into account, but he does not consider the cost of anger, anxiety, and boredom. (Eds.)

IX

SCIENCE TEACHING*

[A DETAILED description of the science program covers the physical facilities, the curriculum, and the methods of teaching. The formal tests used to evaluate achievement in science are described. The summary of the science evaluation follows.]

Gary has . . . shown courage and resourcefulness in trying to deprive science teaching of its remote and abstract character, in trying to bring it into touch with the child's experience and to relate it to his other school work. Teachers of English and teachers of science occasionally attack a large problem together; the shop and the laboratories are at times brought to bear on identical problems. This is excellent as far as it goes, and contains the germ from which a rational

*For detailed account, see report on Science Teaching, by Otis W. Caldwell. [New York: General Education Board, 1918 (Eds.)]

course in school science may ultimately be worked out. But it is not enough merely to break away from the formal, cut and dried type of science teaching represented by most textbooks and to introduce concrete problems from time to time. Chaos supervenes unless aims have been sharply defined and the orderly development of laws and principles assured through intelligent and forceful guidance. Beyond a general, and, be it admitted, a sound predilection for the concrete as embodied in the environment and experience of the child, it is impossible to discern at Gary a principle of organization or progression in science teaching. Unquestionably, the children are interested in their science work and derive pleasure from it. But science fulfills its educational mission, not simply by arousing interest in a disconnected series of phenomena or giving pleasure through a disconnected series of experiences, but by cultivating the child's capacity to deal intelligently and vigorously with problems. This ought indeed to be both an interesting and a pleasurable task; but unless it involves order, persistence, and hard work, its educative effect is probably of minor importance only. Unless so presented, science is likely to be a transient diversion rather than a profoundly formative and disciplinary influence in the child's development.[1]

[1]The value assumptions are very clear. Once again, to what extent is pleasure and interest to be weighed against formal discipline? Caldwell pointed out, in this same chapter, that science education around the country was excessively formal and abstract. He felt the results of science teaching were disappointing: Why fault Gary for having achieved interest and pleasure? He, like the other professional educators, seems to want to do the same thing but achieve a different result; when method changes and a new result is achieved, he is distressed. (Eds.)

X

INDUSTRIAL WORK*

WE HAVE stated in a previous chapter that the Gary scheme springs from a thorough analysis of the existing social situation. The truth of this statement is particularly evidenced by the provisions made for industrial work for boys, household arts for girls, and recreation for all.

[The theoretical rationale for industrial work is given, and a brief description of the shop facilities is provided.]

The amount of time given to industrial instruction varies considerably. . . . [The] theoretical schedules hold fairly well for the several classes of a school, but are only loosely followed in actual practice by the different members of a class. . . .

*For detailed account, see report on Industrial Work, by Charles R. Richards. [New York: General Education Board, 1918 (Eds.)]

Whether the frequent departures from schedule are to be interpreted as indicative of flexibility or laxity must depend to some extent on the care taken by the school to ensure intelligent choice. It would be absurd to hold all pupils to the same formula; it does not follow, however, that it is wise to allow children to do what they choose or as they please. . . . Thus viewed, the Gary administration of shop instruction is lax rather than flexible. The uncontrolled preference of the pupil appeared frequently to be the main determining factor in regard to the disposition and extent of the shop periods.[1]

[A detailed description follows of the shop program, the relationships between students and teachers, and the tests evaluating proficiency in shop work.]

It is not easy to express a definite judgment on the type of industrial work carried on in the two large schools. Unquestionably, the reality, the genuineness of shop instruction

[1]The implication that the professional educator knows best is strong here. (Eds.)

based on maintenance work makes an effective appeal to the boy. He is interested in his shop work; he enjoys it. "One gains a strong impression," writes Professor Richards, "that at Gary school is not a secondary thing in the boy's life, but that it is the big thing. To this attitude of mind the shop work contributes an important element. The shops themselves, although conducted with considerable freedom, generally reflect an atmosphere of real work, and the pupils are often found successfully carrying on operations and achieving results ordinarily judged quite beyond the capacity of boys of their age. The relations between the boys and the instructors are for the most part satisfactory and commendable. The instructors as a rule show much patience in directing the boys, helping them out of difficulties, and answering their many questions. In some of the shops there is much true comradeship between the boys and the instructors built on mutual confidence and respect. Furthermore, the pupils undoubtedly gain a first hand contact with many real phases of industry, and a healthy stimulation of interest through dealing with real problems and real quantities. All this means a vitality and educative influence far superior to the conventional manual training."

On the other hand, the work is narrow in scope, empirical in method. Urgent demands to make this or that repair block instruction; the execution of orders may leave little time for discussion of principles involved or of the methods by which similar tasks are disposed of in current industrial and commercial practice. In some shops, indeed, the artisan-instructor is at times called away and the pupils left for the time without guidance. The limitations pointed out do not, however, affect all shops equally. Plumbing suffers most seriously; in the forge shop, foundry, sheet metal, and particularly in the printing shop, where the entire class is often at work on one job or several similar jobs, group or individual instruction is feasible.

To instruction on the basis of maintenance and repair, there is the further objection that the opportunities which are thus developed are not necessarily those that are of the highest educational value. . . .

The shop men are themselves doubtless under the impression that they are constantly giving instruction, because they are continuously called on for directions and explanations. But the truth is that instruction in a large sense has not been a part of the serious business of the department. The pupils take no notes; no tests of shop or industrial information have been made; no practical correlations of shop experience with mathematics or science work were observed; no charts or sketches on the blackboard are employed; trade catalogues, abounding in illustrative matter, have been used only to a very limited extent.[2] In some cases, it is hardly an overstatement to say that the shop work represents a maximum of activity with a minimum of thought as to the thing done. In part, these defects are ascribable to the employment of artisan teachers; but they could undoubtedly be more or less fully remedied by adequate supervision. . . .[3]

[2]Note the problem: Good work is achieved; the relationship between child and teacher is excellent, but the teachers are not professional and do not use the "correct" professional methods. (Eds.)

[3]Supervision again. The supervisor asserts the importance of supervision without any thought of the human cost of supervision that stultifies the teacher's spirit. It is not self-evident that all supervision is good supervision, or even helpful. (Eds.)

XI

HOUSEHOLD ARTS*

[THE THEORETICAL rationale for the household arts is given. A brief description of the work in the school cafeteria is provided. The teachers are described as are the curriculum and methods for teaching cooking and sewing.]

A single or simple verdict on the instruction in cooking at Gary is impossible, for there are two sides to almost every one of its characteristic features. For example, the introduction of domestic arts into the lower grades through the helper system revives in a measure the wholesome participation of the child in the activities of the home — an order now all too rapidly passing away. But the helper system, as has been pointed out in other connections, is not free from dangers and drawbacks.

*For detailed account, see report on Household Arts, by Eva W. White. [New York: General Education Board, 1918 (Eds.)]

Children cannot really gain unless they are helping older persons who fully understand what they are engaged in doing. Too often the older girls do not measure up to this standard. The instructors labor therefore at a threefold task — they guide the older girls, their proper task, keep the helpers out of mischief, and must have the school luncheon ready at the stroke of eleven. Under this burden the capable instructor becomes discouraged; the weak instructor solves the problem by turning over to the practical cook the preparation of the important dishes.

So also the cafeteria. Much is to be said in its favor. Pupils learn to work with proper regard for time, to handle quantities, to consider money values, to contrive dietetic combinations. Thus the cafeteria not only supplies the school lunch, but enlarges the scope of school work in cooking and gives practical point to the child's effort and interest. But danger lurks in the division of responsibility. One and the same individual at one and the same time teaches cooking and conducts a commercial enterprise; few persons are equally interested and equally effective in both fields. When, for example, the instructor's attention inclines to the commercial side, the pupil suffers. Little or no risk can be taken with the food, for the quantities are large and the hour approaches. The practical cook therefore scarcely realizes how often she prompts the pupil or does things for them; nor does the teacher realize how small a part of the responsibility for the menu is borne by the children. The theory that children must learn to cook by cooking is sound. But, in practice, the importance of the interests at stake seriously infringes on educational independence. In the main, the exigencies of the situation tie the pupils to recipes—paid helpers and instructors constantly aiding even when recipes are followed. So wedded are the pupils to recipes that they are well nigh helpless without them.

Practical and written individual tests were given to pupils in the higher elementary grades in order to ascertain what they could do and with what degree of intelligence. They were asked, for example, to cook potatoes, to bake a cake, to prepare a salad or dessert. In a majority of cases, the results were satisfactory, except for the fact that all the pupils used recipes, failures occurring even under these conditions. Written questions requiring the pupils to explain some of the fundamental principles of good housekeeping . . . were for the most part meagerly answered. . . .

In this respect the same defects were revealed as were remarked by Professor Richards in the industrial work. Obviously, the mere doing of concrete tasks does not carry the pupil far enough to answer legitimate educational requirements. . . .

What now of the sewing? Instruction in sewing at Gary centers around the practical needs of the children. Accordingly, no course of study is mapped out. Pupils work on what they want or need to make; or on garments suggested by parents. . . .[1]

There is no doubt that sewing instruction in the past has erred by too close application to the A, B, C's of technique, and by devoting too much time to drill on valueless objects. Gary has done well to break away from this lock step procedure. But in attempting to

[1]Note how the school program involves the parents in its work.

construct a course in sewing around personal and family needs, it is quite possible that Gary has gone to the other extreme.

The Gary work in sewing assumes that the reality of the task assures the child's interest and that, as compared with this, logical sequence in the tasks set is of inferior importance. The proposition cannot, however, be accepted in this simple form. While the older model exercises have been rightly banished, some form of regular progress is unquestionably indispensable. It is the teacher's business to advance the child more or less regularly through the main steps of plain sewing, dressmaking, and millinery, with constant regard at each step for what is possible. Ability to do things and to do them well is desirable, but it is also important that children give attention to the kind and character of the garments required for different purposes, to the worth and quality of different fabrics, to dyes, and to a multitude of other matters essential to the proper clothing of a modern family. . . .

In the first place, the standard of accomplishment is by no means high. . . . While it is true that trade work and school instruction differ, still, in so far as the processes are common, the home making standard should equal the trade standard. Gary certainly judges its products more leniently than does the trade.

. . . On the whole, however, it remains true that sufficient drill is not given in the principles of garment making, nor is the power to think, as applied to sewing and garment construction, satisfactorily developed.

Two written tests were given high school students to ascertain whether the explanatory and supplementary instruction was sufficient to make the practical work intelligible. . . . The pupils did reasonably well with questions calling for facts and for information related closely to their experiences, but they were weak when the questions called for general information or reasoned answers. . . .

In the household arts as in the industrial work, Gary's experience shows that mere practical occupation is not alone broadly educative. There are indeed physical, social, and intellectual values in these practical activities; but the values do not spontaneously and necessarily accrue to the individual workers. Rather they require to be developed, and therein lies the opportunity for the trained teacher and supervisor.[2]

[2]The value conflicts in the evaluative study are clearly expressed in this section. Knowing *about* doing is placed on a par with, or above, knowing *how* to do. The professional teacher and supervisor recognize the deficiencies in the professionally taught methods of teaching, but cannot relinquish them. (Eds.)

XII

PHYSICAL TRAINING AND PLAY*

The Gary authorities take a broad view of the place of physical education in modern education, giving to it an emphasis double that of the average American city.

[A description of the physical facilities follows.]

Fifteen physical training teachers, as a whole well equipped, have charge of the "play" activities. . . .

There is also a supervisor, who, in addition to regular teaching duties, has general jurisdiction over all. His supervisory duties are, however, ill defined, and he has neither the time nor the authority to organize and standardize the instruction, with the result that teachers work more or less independently of each other.

*For detailed account, see report on Physical Training and Play, by Lee F. Hanmer. [New York: General Education Board, 1918 (Eds.)]

The staff thus made up covers everything done in physical training. Classroom teachers are not required to give any attention whatever to the subject. There is no marching to and from classes, there are no "setting up" or breathing exercises given in the classrooms, and regular teachers do not concern themselves about posture. Only in the small schools on the outskirts of the city do the teachers in charge attend to the physical training. It is possible that here and there a classroom teacher, prompted by personal interest in good posture and right physical development, may give some drill in proper walking, standing, and sitting, but no teacher is expected or required to do so. The physical education of the children, therefore, centers almost exclusively in the gymnasium, swimming pool, and playground.

[The chapter goes on to describe the load the physical education instructors carry, and the varied class sizes.]

Under these conditions, exercises and games suited to each of the different age and grade groups cannot be given. Consequently, "free play" predominates, dangerously near to the exclusion of everything else. This "free play" is of an aimless, running about, and "fooling" character that has little value except as a means of "letting off steam" and stimulating blood circulation — both of which are desirable, but may be secured incidentally in connection with a more constructive use of play time. Even in the brief periods of calisthenic exercises it is not unusual to see several pupils standing idly in their places or taking the exercises listlessly and incorrectly. Snappy, vigorous work is not insisted upon. Hence, much of the physical value of the exercise is lost and the habit of doing work in a slipshod manner is formed. The general aspect of playground and gymnasium suggests, indeed, not school training, aiming to bring about definite results, but rather the more or less unorganized, though in itself wholesome, play appropriate to public playgrounds.

[Some criticism is made of the adequacy of records, and of physical examinations.]

The most systematic work seems to be done in the swimming pools, to which all classes go at regular intervals. The children are taught to swim and dive, and tests of skill and speed add zest and interest to this branch of the work. Life saving and first aid are also taught and well mastered by drill. Very little use is made of group leaders, although much might be done in this way in handling the large numbers.

At times efforts are made to correlate the activities of the play periods with the academic work. . . . Much playground apparatus has been made in the school shops and installed by the children under the direction of the physical training teacher. Equipment thus secured seems to be more highly appreciated, and added interest is undoubtedly given to the shop work.

For some years certain physical tests for elementary and secondary school boys have been used quite generally throughout the United States. They are known as the athletic badge tests. . . . These tests have been accepted and used so generally that the Playground and Recreation Association of

America has prepared bronze badges to be awarded to boys who pass all three tests in either group, in order to encourage boys to bring themselves up to a fair standard of physical development.

[Some details of comparative performance in these tests are given.]

Thus, in twenty one possible comparisons the Gary boys excel in only two instances. How far this poor showing may be due to the presence of newcomers, we do not know.

The ability to jump, run, and pull up are not, however, absolutely conclusive indices of general health conditions and all around bodily vigor. Other ways of reaching conclusions on this phase of the Gary school product were sought. The children were observed at their play and in their athletics to determine the effect of strenuous and prolonged activity. It was plainly evident that they were not easily fatigued. Both boys and girls were able to compete in such vigorous and lengthy events as potato races, obstacle races, sack races, basketball and volley ball, without undue exhaustion and with well sustained vigor. This conclusion was borne out by the scores in basketball games with teams from other cities. Practically without exception the scores for Gary mounted up rapidly in the last half of the playing period, indicating comparatively strong power of endurance. Also when "time out" was called and the visiting players would drop to the floor or the benches for a bit of rest, the Gary team would invariably practise passing the ball and shooting baskets.

Comparatively low markings in the tests with simultaneous evidence of a high degree of bodily vigor are not the results that would naturally be expected.[1] But the freedom allowed the children and the absence of requirements of exactitude and finish in their work, coupled with the generous amount of time allotted to play and other forms of physical activity, may easily account for these apparently conflicting results. Which

[1]The contradiction suggesting a lack of validity for the tests is apparent. However, in the full monograph Mr. Hanmer resolved the contradiction by insisting the children should, indeed *must*, do well on tests if they are to have real physical education. (Eds.)

is the more important and whether it is not possible to secure both proficiency and all around bodily vigor are questions open to debate. Certain it is that habits of inexactness and lack of finish in doing work are a serious handicap and that health and strong power of endurance are most valuable assets.

[There is a brief discussion of girls' test performances. Hanmer goes on to indicate that the large number of pupils in instruction groups makes it impossible to give attention to individual needs.]

The result is an excessive use of free play, which too often is hardly more than an aimless running about and scuffling, without definite aim or results. This type of recreation cannot be fully justified on the theory that the schools treat the gymnasiums and playgrounds as public play spaces, although it is true that the long school day includes some of the time children usually have for free play. Such an attitude is well enough for out of school hours, when, undoubtedly, unorganized play on the school grounds is far better for the child than running the streets. But this is not a sound reason for making a similar use of all school time. Satisfactory bodily training and the cure of individual physical defects cannot be obtained in that way.[2]

[2]Over and over again the professional values of the educator are inserted and employed to evaluate what is observed, and without question. Those of us who have been exposed to professional physical education may have a different viewpoint. How should one weigh the fun of free play against the potential benefits of a planned physical education program when the cost of the latter might well be hatred of the enforced drudgery of formal training programs, and hatred of school? (Eds.)

XIII

AUDITORIUM AND RELIGIOUS INSTRUCTION

[The first part of the chapter presents the theory of the auditorium, describes its facilities, discusses the management of the auditorium program by teachers, and shows how the auditorium is used in the daily schedule.]

At its best, the auditorium is a forum where a pupil, a group, a teacher, or an outsider may make a definite presentation of one kind or another to a fairly homogeneous, interested, self-controlled audience of school children. Here, for example, is a group of, say, 250 children, who, entering the hall in an easy but orderly manner, sit buzzing and expectant — like a mature audience — until the teacher in charge rises and by her presence on the platform procures complete quiet. The preliminaries take place without incident. To-day the feature of the program is a discussion of swimming by the high school girl who, under the direction of the English teacher, had prepared an elaborate and highly creditable memorandum on that subject; to-morrow a high school boy will expound the comparative merits of different automobiles from the salesman's point of view; on another occasion the subject of folk dancing will be presented with illustrative dances prepared by the teacher of physical training. Again, an industrial film — the process of hat making, for example — is exhibited and explained; or a travel film, touching countries whose history or literature has been studied in regular class work. A vigorous and telling address by a demonstrator of the International Harvester Company on the topic "Swat the Fly" fills one day; musical or dramatic numbers fill the next; again, a science class makes a demonstration of their work on the subject of liquid air; an outdoor group does the same for their bird work, or their playground activities.

So much for the auditorium at its best. At its worst, the auditorium simply consumes an hour of the child's time, alternately boring and amusing him with material of little or no educative value because it is either inherently insignificant or poorly done. Much of the work, especially in the smaller schools, is of this sort. Here, for example, an inferior film is run off without comment by a listless teacher to a group of children whose pennies already procure them too much diversion of precisely this kind; again, a group of a dozen children mount the platform to give a poor exhibition in reading to an audience that has nothing to gain even were the performance a good one. At times more promising material is spoiled by lack of careful and intelligent preparation; not infrequently an audience ineffectually handled affects the youthful performers disastrously.

[Religious instruction is given very little attention. About 15 per cent. of the public school enrollment took part in released time religious instruction. Flexner and Bachman mention the issue of separation of church and state briefly, but they express no strong opinion.]

XIV

ENROLLMENT, ATTENDANCE AND PUPIL PROGRESS

The purpose of the public school is to pass every child of the community through a complete elementary, if not a high school course. As yet no system of public schools has by any means realized this purpose. The extent to which a given system succeeds is indicated (1) by its success in enrolling the children, (2) by their attendance, and (3) by their progress through the schools. . . .

The compulsory school period in Indiana ends with the pupil's fourteenth birthday. Any child is legally free to leave school the moment he reaches fourteen. . . .

After six, the public, private, and parochial schools together reach practically all children up to fourteen, about a fifth going to private and parochial schools. But the attracting power of both public and other schools wanes decidedly with children fourteen and over. Still, the Gary schools seem to be unusually successful in attracting children fourteen and fifteen years of age, who are beyond the compulsory attendance age, as they enroll 67 per cent. of the former and 44 per cent of the latter. But that

20 out of each 100, fourteen years of age,

48 out of each 100, fifteen years of age,

70 out of each 100, sixteen years of age,

83 out of each 100, seventeen years of age, and

87 out of each 100, eighteen years of age, should be out of school altogether shows unsatisfactory conditions at Gary[1] as is the case in the country at large.

But mere enrollment is not enough. Pupils must also be held to continuous and regular attendance. Whether or not they are thus held can be inferred, in the first instance, from the number dropping out before completing the course.

[1]Flexner and Bachman are taking into account only the day school. The Gary night school was very popular and served the educational needs of many who dropped out of day school to work. The steel mills, the major employer in Gary, did not employ anyone under sixteen years old. The holding power of the schools over those under age sixteen may have been influenced as much by United States Steel's policies as by the attractiveness of the school program. (Eds.)

Few school systems have complete data either as to the number dropping out or as to the age and grade at which they drop out, and the data at Gary are altogether inadequate on these points. Nevertheless, from such data as are available, the proportion of the enrollment dropping from the Gary schools during the school year appears to be somewhat smaller than is common. . . .

[Comparative data on school dropout rates in several different cities are presented.]

Again, the holding power of the schools is indicated by regularity of attendance. . . . We need to know . . . the regularity of attendance on the part of children actively on the roll a given length of time. . . . Regularity of attendance when so computed runs for the Gary system as a whole as high as 90 per cent. and as low as 86, with 89 per cent. for 1915–16. That children should be out of school after they enroll slightly more than a tenth of the time is not unusual.

Three facts in this connection are worthy of note: First, despite the differences among the several schools in facilities and programs, and despite the differences in nationality and economic status of the children, the per cent. of attendance varies little from school to school, and in no case is it far from the record for the city as a whole.[2] Second, children entering school late attend, when once they are enrolled, about as regularly as those in school from the beginning, an indication probably that the late entrants are mostly newcomers and not truant children. Finally, children living in Gary appear to enter school mostly on the opening day, and the number entering at each later ten day interval does not seem large enough to disturb the progress of school work.

[The problem of measuring age-grade progression is discussed.]

[2]This finding seems to us to be quite remarkable, in view of the fact that the different schools served neighborhoods that were quite different ethnically and in terms of social class. Without having the evidence on hand, we would question whether such regularity of attendance would characterize schools serving diverse neighborhoods in our present-day cities. Either the Gary schools were highly attractive to children from lower-class homes, or attitudes toward education and school attendance correlated differently with social class then and today. (Eds.)

When compared with other cities, Gary is doing as well as they do, but probably no better, in advancing children through the school.[3]

[Detailed data concerning retardation in grade are presented for Gary and other cities.]

Among the favorable factors is the promotion of children three times a year, as well as during term time whenever a child can do the work of the next grade; also the Saturday and summer schools. Saturday is not a regular school day, but the buildings are open and instructors are on duty. Pupils who are falling behind, or who have been absent, or who wish to make two grades in one year, come voluntarily for one or more hours' assistance from their regular weekday teachers. The summer school serves the same end, and is even more effective than the Saturday school

[3]It is our opinion that Flexner and Bachman severely underestimated the influence of the foreign population when comparing Gary with other cities. Few American cities had as high a proportion of first-generation children as Gary, and few had the problems of transiency and the lack of social organization that characterized the newly built city of Gary for many years. (Eds.)

in helping over age children to catch up, weak children to make their grade, and ambitious ones to advance more rapidly than their class. . . .

To conclude, whether the advancement of the Gary children through the schools is measured by their present age-grade status or by their progress after taking up school work at Gary, the Gary schools make a creditable showing, particularly if the foreign character of the population is considered and account is taken of the large number of children coming from other systems. But the two measures employed show only whether children have or have not advanced regularly for their age and for their time in school. They shed no light whatever upon educational performance or achievement.

XV

COSTS*

[IN THIS chapter, the authors present data that summarize total expenditures, and per capita expenditures for the Gary Schools as a whole, and for the Emerson, Froebel, and Jefferson schools separately. They also discuss the degree to which the shops and projects are self-supporting. The following paragraph is their overall summary and evaluation.]

The foregoing discussion makes plain that there is no point in considering school expenditures unless at the same time one considers the return in educational advantages. If one has in mind the Gary plan as embodied in the Froebel and Emerson schools, it is obvious that the plan is not cheap in the sense that its enormously increased oppor-

*For detailed account, see report on Costs, by Frank P. Bachman and Ralph Bowman. [New York: General Education Board, 1918; also G. D. Strayer and F. P. Bachman, *Organization and Administration* (New York: General Education Board, 1918) (Eds.)]

tunities cost actually less than the more limited opportunities of the old red schoolhouse. Of course they cost more, much more, and it is infinitely to its credit that Gary has made the greater investment to achieve the larger purpose. The real question, however, is whether or not the Gary plan costs more for what it gives — whether identical opportunities would cost less on some other plan. For the detailed evidence bearing on this crucial point the reader must consult the technical discussions contained in the volumes on Costs and Organization and Administration. Suffice it here to restate the conclusion there expressed, that, though additional data are desirable, it appears that schools organized on the Gary plan promise an extended and enriched course of study at minimum cost. In other words, the advantages offered by the Gary schools at their best probably cost less than the same advantages on a more conventional plan of school organization.

XVI

CONCLUSION

In bringing this volume to a close, it is perhaps worth while to sum up briefly the pros and cons of a complicated situation.

On the credit side of the ledger must be placed the fact that Gary has adopted, and taken effective steps towards providing facilities for, a large and generous conception of public education. Had Gary played safe, we should find there half a dozen or more square brick "soap-box" buildings, accommodating a dozen classes, each pursuing the usual book studies, a playground, with little or no equipment, perhaps a basement room for manual training, a laboratory, and a cooking room for girls. Provided with this commonplace system, the town would have led a conventional school life — quiet, unoffending, and negatively happy — doing as many others do, doing it about as well as they do it, and satisfied to do just that. Instead, it adopted the progressive, modern conception of school function, formulated its conception in clear terms and with all possible expedition provided facilities adequate to the conception. The adoption and execution of this policy required administrative courage and civic liberality. In one sense there was nothing revolutionary in it, for not a few schoolmen have adopted this broad conception of public education. But Gary not only adopted this conception in theory — it made realization possible by providing in its main schools the physical conditions needed for its execution. The Froebel and the Emerson schools are not simply fine buildings, that in their environment startle the visitor — they are instruments formed to embody and realize a distinct educational idea. Even the temporary makeshifts required by the exigencies of the situation show an intelligent and serious effort to do what is feasible in the same direction for children unable to attend the well equipped central schools. The extended curriculum is therefore a reality at Gary, and the general movement toward enrichment of the curriculum has been greatly stimulated by Gary's example.

On the credit side of the ledger belongs also Gary's contribution to school organization. There can be no question that a modern plant, consisting of classrooms, shops, gymnasium, laboratories, and auditorium, can be operated on the Gary type of organization so as to accommodate a considerably larger number of children than the same plant operated on the conventional plan. Indeed, the Gary type of organization anticipates such unsatisfactory and deplorable make-shifts, as "part time," by providing on purely educational grounds for the intensive use of all school facilities. Thus, without waiting to be driven by pressure of large numbers, Gary has developed a type of school organization which permits the effective instruction of the maximum number of children in a plant having modern facilities. From this point of view, the Gary organization is perhaps the most fruitful suggestion yet contributed toward the practical solution of the administrative problems involved in realizing a broad conception of public education.

Finally, Gary has attempted to practise democratic theory in school conduct and discipline. It is a commonplace that arbitrary or military discipline is alien to the American spirit. Coöperation, representing the willing subordination of the individual in the endeavor to achieve necessary and desirable ends, must somehow be procured. In various ways — in classroom, corridors, auditorium, shop, etc. — Gary appeals to the coöperative spirit, relies on it, believes in it, gives it something to do — at times perhaps unwisely and to excess. In any event, the schools are rich in color and movement, they are places where children live as well as learn, places where children obtain educational values, not only through books, but through genuine life activities. The Gary schools make a point not only of the well known measurable abilities, but of happiness and appreciation, which cannot be measured, even though they may be sensed. It does not follow that Gary obtains no results from these efforts, merely because the outcome of its efforts in classroom work is unsatisfactory. The final results of appreciation and stimulus are too subtle, too remote, too readily obscured or augmented by other factors in experience or environment to be themselves definitely appraised. But evidence that appeal to the appreciative instincts is not made in vain is encountered now here, now there, in the activities, interests, and attitudes of teachers and children alike.

There are, it is clear, two distinct bodies to material employed at Gary, each having its appropriate method of approach: first, definite subjects, that have in the last resort to be "learned" in such wise that the pupil may attain and demonstrate a reasonable degree of mastery; next, æsthetic or other activities, giving wholesome pleasure at the time and tending to establish higher levels of need and taste. The traditional pedagogue concentrates on the first group and relentlessly organizes the subjects contained within it. The philosopher, insisting that at its best education supplies the means of natural growth, emphasizes the second group, not infrequently revolting from systematic presentation and precise results.[1] A really effective school will undoubtedly harmonize

[1]Certainly a contemporary problem in higher education where a trend is developing to give college credits for here-and-now experiences, frequently divorced from any requirement of an intellectual product. (Eds.)

the two. It will set up high and definite standards of workmanship for tasks that represent desired skills — spelling, arithmetic, cooking, sewing, or what not — endeavoring to reach these by employing well thought out and well wrought out methods of procedure; it will also provide a variety of experiences of a stimulating and appreciative character, without being overmuch concerned at the moment to decide why they are good, or what good they do, then or thereafter. One gets at Gary the impression of confusion in this matter. The auditorium, for example, embodies largely the stimulating and appreciative experiences that cannot be closely followed up. But the type of procedure that is natural to the auditorium not infrequently invades the shops, the cafeteria, and the classrooms, as if the passive absorption adapted to the auditorium were a generally applicable educational method.

We thus pass to the debit side of the account. The readers of this volume already know that the execution of the Gary plan is defective. It is of course true that no public school system thus far critically studied has been pronounced satisfactory — satisfactory in the sense that it meets current and reasonable standards of efficiency. It would therefore be manifestly unfair to demand that Gary should fully embody and practically succeed with every item of its varied and extensive program. A good many extenuating considerations may be fairly urged — the newness of the community, the complexities due to the character of the population, the breadth of the conception, the enormous difficulty of obtaining a teaching and supervising staff competent to execute the plan. But after making every possible allowance, it remains to be admitted that in respect to administration and instruction Gary might fairly have been expected to make a better showing.

Fundamentally, the defect is one of administration. No scheme will execute itself. Precisely because the Gary scheme is complicated, extensive, and at some points novel, uncommonly watchful administrative control is requisite. Such control does not exist. In consequence, results appear to be largely taken for granted. Illustrations in proof of this statement may be drawn from many of the preceding chapters. For example, the present organization assumes that satisfactory educational results are obtained when the plant consists half of regular classrooms and half of special facilities, and these facilities are kept in continuous use. As the plan works out, the groups assembled at Gary in the auditorium or on the playground are large or small, composed of a single grade or many grades, according to the requirements of a schedule constructed on this basis. It would, of course, be most convenient if this somewhat mechanical arrangement proved educationally effective. But does it? Not, in our judgment, without certain cautions and qualifications which Gary has thus far neglected. The "duplicate" school organization should therefore be viewed as an experiment to be watched and modified rather than assumed as a principle according to which a school schedule may be arbitrarily arranged.

The execution of the Gary plan is again defective in respect to educational supervision.[2] To be sure, teaching and discipline

[2]We have noted the assumption that "good" supervision would have necessarily been effective. (Eds.)

in harmony with the Gary idea are to be found; side by side, however, are also teaching and discipline of old-fashioned type. Of course, this is inevitable. No consistently modern scheme could be completely realized at this time, because the materials have not as yet been created, the teachers have not yet been trained. Criticism is warranted, not because crudities and inconsistencies occur, but because the agencies which ought to be concerned over this situation have failed to take hold of it vigorously. Consequently in the so-called "old line" branches, the fundamental necessities of education, Gary execution falls short of usual performance. In reaching out for something new, Gary has too lightly parted with certain essential and established values, without being aware of the loss it has inadvertently made.

Not even in those branches to which Gary has given impetus and development — the so-called special activities — has a high or even satisfactory standard been reached. An excellent spirit pervaded the playgrounds, gymnasiums, shops, laboratories, and household arts departments. But high — even satisfactory — standards of workmanship did not rule. Some boys and girls did well; some did ill; concerted effort to procure generally good work, conscientious insistence upon excellent performance are only spasmodically in evidence. Not that teachers and principals do not want good work; they plainly do. But that patient and close attention to details by which alone good work can be obtained was far too irregular to be effective. Here, as elsewhere, one cannot avoid the conclusion that a large and generous scheme, distinguished by intelligence and vision in conception, falls too far short in the execution.

Attention has been called to the ways in which pupils participate in responsible activities — record keeping, etc. Such participation is admirably calculated to give a flavor of reality to school life. What ought, however, to be a credit item is converted into a debit because the absence of proper accountability results in slipshod work that must do the pupils positive damage. Records characterized by poor spelling, arithmetical inaccuracies, and grave omissions pass unchallenged. Not only is the immediate educative effect lost, but the child tends to become habituated to inferior performance. Thus, once more sound conception is frustrated by ineffective execution.

Could the Gary scheme be acceptably executed without additional expenditure? If not, how much more would have to be spent? Or can results of higher quality be obtained on the present outlay only by attempting less? We are unable to say. These questions cannot be finally answered until the present administrative and supervisory officers either conceive their functions somewhat differently or exercise them more effectively. Unquestionably, the mere process of gearing up the present organization would substantially improve results; for which reason it would be unwise either to curtail opportunities or largely to increase expenditure until the existing system has shown what it can accomplish when on the alert.

An eminent surgeon, accounting for his success in treating a recalcitránt wound, recently remarked of the hospital with which he is associated: "Here we try things." He did not mean that he and his associates follow a hit-or-miss policy. He was, in point of fact, describing an arduous, rigorous, exacting, and at the same time strictly accountable procedure. They canvass their resources, select in a critical way the moves which may reasonably be expected to prove beneficial, and with the most scrupulous care watch the outcome, determining the next procedure on the basis of ascertained results. They "try things," but they "try things" intelligently and critically.

It is a severe criticism of much of our current education that it does not "try things." This modern world of ours is in many ways a new world, with new peoples facing new problems and new opportunities. We tell ourselves again and again that only through education can safe and happy adjustments be reached; no one pretends that education has yet found these adjustments. Nevertheless, educational inertia is all but invincible. Only here and there in the person of this or that teacher or principal or supervisor does it "try things." And the moment it is proposed to "try things" — the only method by which progress can be made — the forces of conservatism organize to check and discredit progressive enterprise.

It is to the substantial and lasting credit of Gary that it has had the courage, liberality, and imagination to "try things." Nor have things been tried blindly and recklessly. The social situation to be dealt with has been thoughtfully analyzed; the resources at our disposal have been intelligently marshaled. That is, Gary did not act in ignorance of the situation to be met; it did not employ ill adjusted tools. It has failed only in caution and criticism. Hence, while things have been tried, results have not been carefully checked. Disappointment was inevitable, but it is disappointment that does not necessarily imply fundamental error.

It is not difficult to understand why self-criticism was overlooked. Education has for centuries too largely consisted of exercises habitually practised, partly for known and obvious, partly for unknown, ends. It made little practical difference whether the end was known or unknown, because in neither case were schoolmen accustomed to examine results carefully in order to ascertain what their efforts and processes achieved. In failing to scrutinize results, Gary simply did as others did.[3] There is also another consideration. The Gary scheme was conceived in enthusiasm. The temperament of the reformer is not usually associated in the same individual with the temperament of the critic.[4] The two must, however, be brought together. The innovator must formulate his purposes clearly and concretely; and his results must be measured in the light of his professed aims. If innovation is carried on in this critical spirit, conservatism will also have to submit to assay.

The theory of which Gary is an exemplification is derived from the facts and necessities of modern life. The defects of Gary cannot therefore simply throw us back on the meager type of education appropriate enough to other conditions. Gary's experience up to this time means merely that further efforts, at

[3]We still do not have ways of implementing the findings of evaluative studies. For example, Levine and Graziano (in press) present evidence dating back to 1911 that leaving children back in school does no good and may be positively harmful. Children are still left back in school. (Eds.)

[4]This same issue is noted in a discussion of the New Haven, Connecticut antipoverty agency, Community Progress, Incorporated, by Sarason *et al.* (1966).

Gary and elsewhere, more clearly defined, more effectively controlled, must be made in order, if possible, to accomplish Gary's avowed object — the making of our schools adequate to the needs and conditions of current life.[5]

[5]To which nothing further need be added. (Eds.)

REFERENCES

Addams, J. *Twenty Years at Hull House.* New York: Macmillan, 1910.

Bennis, W. G. *Changing Organizations.* New York: McGraw-Hill, 1966.

Bennis, W. G., Benne, K. D., and Chin, R. (Eds.). *The Planning of Change.* New York: Holt, Rhinhart and Winston, 1961.

Bourne, R. S. *Youth and Life.* Boston: Houghton Mifflin, 1913.

Bourne, R. S. "New York and the Gary System." *Educational Administration and Supervision 2* (1916): 284–289.

Bourne, R. S. *Education and Living.* New York: The Century Co., 1917.

Bourne, R. S. *The State.* New York: Resistance Press, 1946–1947.

Bourne, R. S. "Twilight of Intellectuals." In V. W. Brooks (Ed.). *The History of a Literary Radical and Other Papers by Randolph S. Bourne.* New York: S. A. Russell, 1956.

Brooks, V. W. (Ed.). *The History of a Literary Radical and Other Papers by Randolph Bourne.* New York: S. A. Russell, 1956.

Callahan, R. E. *Education and the Cult of Efficiency.* Chicago: University of Chicago Press, 1962.

Claxton, P. P. "Early Days of Platoon Schools." *The Platoon School. 1* (1924): 3.

Cohen, S. *Progressives and Urban School Reform. The Public Education Association of New York City 1895–1954.* New York: Bureau of Publications, Teachers College, Columbia University, 1964.

Cotter, A. *U.S. Steel: A Corporation with a Soul.* Garden City, N.Y.: Doubleday Page, 1921.

Cremin, L. A. *The Transformation of the School.* New York: Knopf, 1961.

Davis, A. F. *Spearheads for Reform: The Social Settlements and the Progressive Movement, 1890–1914.* New York: Oxford University Press, 1967.

Dewey, J. *My Pedagogic Creed.* C. L. Kellogg and Co., 1897.

Dewey, J., and Dewey, E. *Schools of Tomorrow.* New York: E. P. Dutton, 1915.

Escarpit, Robert. *Sociologie de la Littérature.* Paris: Presses Universitaires de France, 1960.

Filler, L. *Randolph Bourne.* Washington, D.C.: American Council on Public Affairs, 1943.

Flexner, A. *A Modern School.* New York: General Education Board, 1916.

Flexner, A. *I Remember: The Autobiography of Abraham Flexner.* New York: Simon and Schuster, 1940.

Flexner, A. *Abraham Flexner: An Autobiography.* New York: Simon and Schuster, 1960.

Goldenberg, I. I. *Build Me a Mountain: Youth, Poverty, and the Creation of New Settings.* Cambridge, Mass.: The M.I.T. Press, 1970.

Gouldner, A. W. "The Sociologist as Partisan: Sociology and the Welfare State." *The American Sociologist 3* (1968): 103–116.

Graziano, A. M. "Clinical Innovation and the Mental Health Power Structure: A Social Case History." *American Psychologist 24* (1969): 10–18.

Gulick, C. A. *Labor Policy of the U.S. Steel Corporation.* Unpublished Ph.D. Thesis, Columbia University, 1924.

Huaco, George. *Sociology of the Novel: Mexico, 1915–1966.* Unpublished manuscript.

Huaco, George. *The Sociology of Film Art.* New York: Basic Books, 1965.

Houghton Mifflin. *Fifty Years of Publishing: The History of the Educational Department of the Houghton Mifflin Company.* Boston: Houghton Mifflin, 1930.

Katz, M. B. *The Irony of Early School Reform.* Cambridge, Mass.: Harvard University Press, 1968.

Lasch, C. *The New Radicalism in America.* New York: Random House, 1965.

Levine, M., and Graziano, A. M. "Intervention Programs in Elementary Schools." In S. Golann and C. Eisdorfer (Eds.). *Handbook of Community Psychology and Mental Health.* New York: Appleton-Century-Crofts (in press).

Levine, M., and Levine, A. *A Social History of Helping Services: Clinic, Court, School and Community.* New York: Appleton-Century-Crofts, 1970.

Lewinson, E. R. *John Purroy Mitchel: The Boy Mayor of New York.* New York: Astra Books, 1965.

Marris, P., and Rein, M. *Dilemmas of Social Reform: Poverty and Community Action in the United States.* New York: Atherton, 1967.

Mills, C. W. *Sociology and Pragmatism.* New York: Oxford University Press, 1964.

Moore, R. A. *The Calumet Region.* Indianapolis: Indiana Historical Bureau, 1959.

Moreau, J. A. *Randolph Bourne: Legend and Reality.* Washington, D.C.: Public Affairs Press, 1966.

Paul, S. *Randolph Bourne.* Minneapolis: University of Minnesota Press, 1966.

Sarason, S. B. *The Culture of the School and the Problem of Change.* Boston: Allyn and Bacon (in press).

Sarason, S. B., Davidson, K. S., and Blatt, B. *The Preparation of Teachers.* New York: Wiley, 1962.

Sarason, S. B., Levine, M., Goldenberg, I. I., Cherlin, D. C., and Bennett, E. M. *Psychology in Community Settings.* New York: Wiley, 1966.

Swift, F. H. "Impressions of the Gary School System." *Educational Administration and Supervision 2* (1916): 503–512.

Tarbell, I. M. *The Life of Elbert H. Gary: A Story of Steel.* New York: D. Appleton and Co., 1926.

Watt, I. *The Rise of the Novel.* Berkeley, Calif: University of California Press, 1962.

INDEX